THE INTERNATIONAL HEYER SOCIETY ANNUAL 2020

Nonpareil #1 - #6
The Weekly Post Vol. I

EDITED BY RACHEL HYLAND

Overlord Publishing

overlordpublishing.com

Copyright Declaration

© 2021 by The International Heyer Society

Our thanks to special guest contributors Sara-Mae Tuson, Rachel Grant, Professor Chris Browne, Clara Shipman, Frances Turner, Heather Wallace, Maura Tan, Kirsten Davis, Colleen Reed, Ruth Williamson and Sally Dale.

All rights reserved. No part of this book may be used or reproduced in in any manner whatsoever without written permission, except in the case of brief quotations embodied in critical articles or reviews.

Overlord Publishing. As was foretold.

Check overlordpublishing.com for news of our other exciting releases.

For all the Heyerites everywhere

Georgette Heyer (1902 - 1974)

ABOUT THE INTERNATIONAL HEYER SOCIETY

Unlike receiving a voucher for Almack's or an invitation to box with Gentleman Jackson, becoming a member of the International Heyer Society is easy! As the name suggests, we welcome members from all over the world, and offer an abundance of perks along with our monthly circular, *Nonpareil,* and the aptly named *Weekly Post*.

Officially launched on July 1, 2020, the Society aims to promote the works of Georgette Heyer throughout the world. Come join us!

HEYERSOCIETY.COM

CONTENTS

2020 MEMBERSHIP ROLL 4
INTRODUCTION 5
NONPAREIL #1 6
FROM THE PATRONESSES
THE BLACK MOTH
THE CHARACTERS
THE LOCATIONS 7
CELEBRITY SIGHTINGS
WHAT A QUIZ!
WHAT THEY SAID
SELECTED COVER GALLERY
ESSAY: THE BLACK MOTH: A REMARKABLE DEBUT

NONPAREIL #2 13
FROM THE PATRONESSES
THE GREAT ROXHYTHE
THE CHARACTERS
THE LOCATIONS
CELEBRITY SIGHTINGS
WHAT A QUIZ!
WHAT THEY SAID
SELECTED COVER GALLERY
ESSAY: ROXHYTHE SYNDROME

NONPAREIL #3 21
FROM THE PATRONESSES
THE TRANSFORMATION OF PHILIP JETTAN
THE CHARACTERS
THE LOCATIONS
CELEBRITY SIGHTINGS
WHAT A QUIZ!
WHAT THEY SAID
SELECTED COVER GALLERY
ESSAY: CLEONE: NAY OR YEA?
  "NAY!" BY RACHEL HYLAND
  "YEA!" BY JENNIFER KLOESTER

NONPAREIL #4 28
FROM THE PATRONESSES
INSTEAD OF THE THORN
THE CHARACTERS
THE LOCATIONS
CELEBRITY SIGHTINGS
WHAT A QUIZ!
SELECTED COVER GALLERY
WHAT THEY SAID
ESSAY: HER FIRST CONTEMPORARY NOVEL

NONPAREIL #4 35
FROM THE PATRONESSES
SIMON THE COLDHEART
THE CHARACTERS
CELEBRITY SIGHTINGS
THE LOCATIONS
WHAT THEY SAID
SELECTED COVER GALLERY
ESSAY: SIMON THE [INSERT NICKNAME HERE]
WHAT A QUIZ!

NONPAREIL #5 42
FROM THE PATRONESSES
THESE OLD SHADES
THE CHARACTERS
CELEBRITY SIGHTINGS
THE LOCATIONS
WHAT A QUIZ
WHAT THEY SAID
SELECTED COVER GALLERY
ESSAY: THESE OLD SHADES: A HISTORY
WHAT A QUIZ!

THE WEEKLY POST, VOL I. 52
#1 - FINDING HEYER BY RACHEL HYLAND 52
#2 - LADY JERSEY BY SUSANNAH FULLERTON 53
#3 - LADY SEFTON BY JENNIFER KLOESTER 54
#4 - THE MAKING OF THE MOST EPIC (WELL, AT LEAST THE FIRST) GEORGETTE HEYER PODCAST! BY SARA-MAE TUSON 56
#5 – COUNTESS LIEVEN BY RACHEL HYLAND 57
#6 – TOURING WITH GEORGETTE HEYER BY SUSANNAH FULLERTON 59
#7 – MAYFAIR PET ADOPTION AGENCY BY RACHEL GRANT 60
#8 – IN PURSUIT OF THE DUST JACKET OF *THE BLACK MOTH* BY PROFESSOR CHRIS BROWNE 61
#9 – THE TRANSFORMATION OF PHILIP JETTAN: THE FINAL CHAPTER 62
#10 – A MATTER OF URGENCY BY SUSANNAH FULLERTON
#11 – YOU'RE MUCH TOO YOUNG, GIRL BY CLARA SHIPMAN 67
#12 – GEORGE HEYER: POET AND PLAYWRIGHT BY JENNIFER KLOESTER 69
#13 – "THE ROMANCE OF A CARPET BEATING" BY GEORGE HEYER 70
#14 – "VISIONS" BY GEORGE HEYER 72
#15 – TWO SHORT POEMS BY GEORGE HEYER 75
#16 – JACKO BY RACHEL GRANT 76
#17 – MY TOP TEN HEYER HEROINES BY RACHEL HYLAND
#18 – MY TOP TEN HEYER HEROES BY RACHEL HYLAND 79
#19 – YOUR TOP TEN HEYER HEROINES AND HEROES 82
#20 – SUCH AN AMUSING VILLAIN – HEYER'S BAD GUYS BY CLARA SHIPMAN 85
#21 – WHY CLORINDA? BY SUSANNAH FULLERTON 86
#22 – LOCATION, LOCATION, LOCATION IN HEYER BY CLARA SHIPMAN 87
#23 – CHRISTMAS IN HEYER'S REGENCY BY RACHEL HYLAND 88
#24 – CHRISTMAS PUDDING BY SUSANNAH FULLERTON
#25 – THE CHRISTMAS GIFT BY GEORGETTE HEYER 91

AFTER GEORGETTE 93
THE READING ROOM 95
GEORGETTE HEYER'S BIBLIOGRAPHY 96

2020 MEMBERSHIP ROLL

Peta Allen
Amelia Autin
Jan Avent
Lori Bailey
Sue Baillie
Josephine Bayne
Diane Beck
Ricky Berghofer
Laura Boon
Melinda Borrell
Charlotte Brothers
Becky Brown
Rachel Brown
Chris Browne
Linda Brumley
Vanessa Buck
Ann Burns
Linda Carmichael
Anne Carpenter
Mercia Chapman
Janice Clemson
Elizabeth Collins
Elizabeth Collison
Angela Connell
Geraldine Connor
Samuel Costello
Elizabeth Cowan
Glenda Cooper
Patricia Costello
Danielle Crowley
Sarah Crowley
Sonia Cruickshank
Sally Dale
Helen Davidge
Kirsten Davis
Annette Dent
Anne Dunn
Jay Dixon
Kitty Estopinal
Mary Fagan
Nancy Flitcroft
Barbara Freedman
R Cinthia Garcia Soria
Laura George
Donna Gilbert
Cynthia Glenney
Kerrin Glover
Kathleen Glancy

Bridget Godwin
Suzanne Gotro
Rachel Grant
Heather Gray
Terry Gray
Kerrie Gribble
Heather Grove
Jenny Haddon
Gillian Hanhart
Jo Harris
Audrey Harrison
Sarah Harvey
Johanna Henwood
Heather Higgs
Sally Houghton
Kelly Howsley-Glover
Diane Hughes
Elizabeth Hughes
Anne Hurst Hardock
Philippa Hutton
Lucy Huntzinger
Ruth Hyland
Kristin Jensen
Amanda Jones
Harriet Jordan
Patricia Keith
Megan Kemmis
Julia Kelly
Justine Lee
Lucretia Lee
Vicki Liberman
Jill Livingstone
Susan Mackenzie
Rebekah Manson
Isolde Martyn
Tamar McKenzie-Smith
Heather McNeill
Brigitta Merchant
Kirsten Merchant
Sharon Micenko
Carolyn Miller
Margo Moore
Maryanne Moore
Margaret Morgan
Susann Morgan
Kym Morris
Jacinta O'Keefe
Joan Sheedy

Julie O'Keefe
Megan Osmond
Peta Parr
Lynne Parrott
Betsy Payne
Joanna Penglase
Yvonne Powell
Roslyn Power
Colleen Reed
Norreida Reyes
Elda Ribeiro
Sharon Roberts
Keryne Rosato
Cathleen Ross
Mark Robinson
Marsha Shannon
D Shepherd
Claire Shevlin
Clara Shipman
Adam Simon
Graham Sims
Kathy Skok
Joanne Smith
Christine Stinson
Rosemary St John
Pamela Staples
Margaret Sullivan
Miranda Spatchurst
Maura Tan
Felicity Taylor
Kiera Tchelistcheff
Sara-Mae Tuson
Frances Turner
Sue Vickers-Thompson
Frances Walker
Selina Walker
Jacqueline Weidman
D. Williams
Ruth Williamson
Heather Wallace
Karin Westman
Sara Wisnia
Malvina Yock
Zoe Younger
Katherine Zimmerman

A Lady (x 5)
A Gentleman (x 2)

Patronesses: Rachel Hyland
Jennifer Kloester
Susannah Fullerton

INTRODUCTION

For those of us in the know, Georgette Heyer's novels are a guarantee of many pleasurable hours spent in the worlds she created, with characters who live for the reader, witty dialogue to make you laugh aloud and such clever, often intricate plots, that one must keep on reading until the final imbroglio is played out.

Heyer's fifty-six novels span three genres: contemporary fiction, detective fiction and historical fiction. It is for this last that she is best known, although her detective fiction also has a strong following among those who love the 'Golden Age' writers of that genre. It was in her historical fiction, however, that Georgette Heyer struck gold.

Her first novel, an eighteenth-century romance, was published in 1921, her first Regency novel was published in 1935; from 1944 until her death thirty years later, and with just two exceptions, she wrote only Regency novels. Inspired by Jane Austen and writing her own brand of ironic comedy, with those twenty-six novels Georgette Heyer created a genre – the Regency. Today, more than forty years after her death, Heyer is still read and loved around the world and there is increasing interest in this reclusive bestselling author.

When, early in 2020, Rachel Hyland suggested we create the International Heyer Society I was in alt (as a Heyer character would say). Here, fans both old and new could discover more about Georgette Heyer, her life, her writing and her books and with this elegant, open and inclusive platform, we could discuss aspects of the writer and her work not yet explored.

Today, I am honoured to be one of the three Patronesses of the International Heyer Society in company with my esteemed companions: the brilliant, Susannah Fullerton OAM, FRSN, and president of the Jane Austen Society of Australia, and the inimitable Rachel Hyland, editor, author and publisher. As Lady Jersey, Princess Lieven and Lady Sefton, we three are delighted to present for our members' delectation the first International Heyer Society Annual, which we hope you will dip into, savour and enjoy.

Here's to an even richer year in 2021 and may we celebrate the great Miss Heyer's centenary in style!

– *Jennifer Kloester*
Geelong, 2021

**JOIN THE INTERNATIONAL HEYER SOCIETY AT
HEYERSOCIETY.COM**

NONPAREIL

International Heyer Society Circular #1, July 2020

FROM THE PATRONESSES

Welcome to the International Heyer Society!

In this, the very first edition of our monthly circular *Nonpareil*, we are discussing Georgette Heyer's first novel, *The Black Moth*. From the characters to the locations to contemporary reviews and more, we delve deep into the lore of this most important and impressive of debuts.

> "In love? You? Nonsense! Nonsense! Nonsense! You do not know what the word means. You are like a—like a fish, with no more love in you than a fish, and no more heart than a fish, and—"
>
> "Spare me the rest, I beg. I am very clammy, I make no doubt, but you will at least accord me more brain than a fish?"
>
> — *The Black Moth*, Chapter VI

> "... if your passion is love, 'tis a strange one that puts yourself first. I would not give a snap of a finger for it! You want this girl, not for her happiness, but for your own pleasure. That is not the love I once told you would save you from yourself. When it comes, you will count yourself as naught; you will realise your own insignificance, and above all, be ready to make any sacrifice for her sake."
>
> — *The Black Moth*, Chapter XIX

THE BLACK MOTH

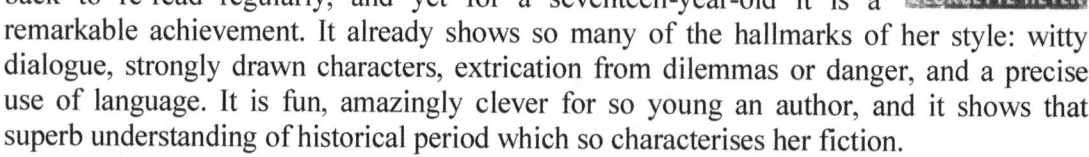

THE Juvenilia Press publishes the early works of writers who went on to become famous, categorizing 'juvenilia' as "youthful writing up to the ages of twenty" — so Georgette Heyer's *The Black Moth* fits in very nicely. Most of what they publish is either 'lost' or unpublished, but not so with *The Black Moth*, which is nearing 100 years of continuous publication.

It is far from my favourite Heyer novel and I find it is not one I go back to re-read regularly, and yet for a seventeen-year-old it is a remarkable achievement. It already shows so many of the hallmarks of her style: witty dialogue, strongly drawn characters, extrication from dilemmas or danger, and a precise use of language. It is fun, amazingly clever for so young an author, and it shows that superb understanding of historical period which so characterises her fiction.

I think we can all feel grateful to Georgette's brother, Boris. Had he not listened with rapt attention to her tale, she might well have been discouraged, and then put down her pen. But surely Boris laughed in all the right places and begged for more, and so he gave his sister the encouragement and literary start she needed. In 2021 I will be celebrating the centenary of Georgette Heyer's first novel, partly for itself, but especially because it led to so much more!

— *Susannah Fullerton*

THE CHARACTERS

JOHN "JACK" ANTHONY ST. ERVINE DELANEY CARSTARES, EARL OF WYNCHAM, AKA SIR ANTHONY FERNDALE; JOHN CARR
Falsely accused of cheating at cards, Jack fled Polite Society and, in the intervening six years, at some point became a highwayman. For the fun of it, mostly.

JIM SALTER
The most faithful of valets – among other things it seems there is nothing Jim cannot do – Jim is devoted to Jack and in on the secret of his illegal activities, but not his earldom.

JENNY
The smartest horse in all the land, there is no horse to compare with Jenny. She does almost get Jack arrested, though.

SIR MILES O'HARA
A genial country squire and Justice of the Peace before whom Jack is brought after an ill-fated robbery attempt. Happens to be Jack's best-friend.

MRS. MOLLY O'HARA
A kind-hearted, vivacious and somewhat managing matron, wife to Sir Miles and with a weakness for men with "white hands." Was prepared to lie to her husband for Jack's sake. Matchmaker.

THE HON. RICHARD "DICK" CARSTARES
Jack's brother, and the real perpetrator of the infamous card-cheating incident, Dick is haunted by his misdeeds, and tortured by his selfish wife, whom he won through Jack's sacrifice.

COLONEL DARE
Held the card party at which Dick cheated.

JOHN CARSTARES
Dick's son, neglect3ed by his mother.

BETTY
His nurse.

JIM DAVENANT
Once a friend of Jack's.

LADY LAVINIA CARSTARES
Dick's selfish wife. She is beautiful, vain and prone to histrionics. Sister to the calculating Duke of Andover, she was but a pawn in his game to discredit Jack for his own financial reward. That is no excuse for her subsequent behaviour – especially towards her son.

HUGH TRACY CLARE BELMANOIR, DUKE OF ANDOVER, AKA MR. EVERARD; SIR HUGH GRANDISON
A Machiavellian schemer of the first order, Tracy (as he is known) is a sociopath and a serial abductor of women. He's very witty, though, which seems to make up for it.

LORD ANDREW BELMANOIR
Tracy and Lavinia's scapegrace younger brother, an inveterate, profligate gamester and spendthrift who is yet friend to all. Relies on Dick for financial support.

CAPTAIN LORD ROBERT "BOB" BELMANOIR
The other Belmanoir. No one likes Bob.

THE HON. FRANK FORTESCUE
Tracy's best-friend, a man of principle and good sense, but who just can't seem to quit him, and believes in his ability to be a better man, for some reason.

SIR JOHN FORTESCUE
A dull dog – so, naturally, he is a friend of Dick's. Elder brother of Frank.

CAPTAIN HAROLD LOVELACE
A former love of Lady Lavinia's. The dapper Captain's return to London leads that lady into indiscretion, with her intent to run away from her husband and child.

MRS HARRIET FLEMING
A cousin of the Belmanoirs.

MR WILLIAM FLEMING
Her husband, considered "beneath" her.

LORD FOTHERINGHAM
Tracy's friend; rebuffed by Diana.

HARPER
Employed by Tracy to inveigle himself into Diana's household, and to aid in her abduction.

DIANA BEAULEIGH
Beautiful, determined and unconventional, the gently-bred Diana is an object of much affection, including that of Tracy – who, of course, wants to abduct her – and Jack, who saves her from said abduction. Twice.

ELIZABETH "BETTY" BEAULEIGH
Diana's maiden aunt, a woman of much fortitude. An excellent judge of character.

MR. BEAULEIGH
Diana's ineffective (often indifferent) father.

MR. BETTISON
Local squire, also in love with Diana.

MR. WARBURTON
The Carstares family lawyer and general factotum. Has a deep affection for Jack.

MRS. HESTER THOMPSON
Friend of Miss Betty. Unpleasant company, but generous with her home in Bath.

CHADBER
Keeps the inn at Fallowfield; makes good beer.

MR. CHILTER
A thin and harried clerk, he is taken by the outlaw's kindness during a holdup and lies on his behalf. Later employed by Jack.

MRS. ISABELLA FANSHAWE
A lovely widow newly arrived in London, who once knew Jack on the Continent. She becomes Dick's confidante, much to the displeasure of Lady Fanny.

MR FUDBY
His employer, portly and cantankerous.

MR BRAND
Town clerk of Lewes. Not fond of Mr Fudby.

LORD AVON
Giver of card parties; has a braying laugh.

JACK CHOLMONDLEY
Attends Lord Avon's card party.

LADY CARLYLE
Rival of Lavinia Carstares.

CHEVALIER JULIAN D'EGMONT
Knows all the gossip from the French Court.

SIR DOUGLAS FAVERSHAM
A cisisbeo of Lady Fanny's.

"I'll see what can be done for your protégé, Molly. But don't be forgetting he tried to kill the only husband you have!"
— *The Black Moth*, Chapter IX

"We Belmanoirs are all half-mad," replied Tracy sweetly, "but I think in my case it is merely concentrated evil."
— *The Black Moth*, Chapter VI

THE LOCATIONS

CHEQUERS INN, FALLOWFIELD
~ 50 miles from Lewes
WYNCHAM
~ 35 miles west of Midhurst, across moorland
ANDOVER COURT
7 miles south west of Wyncham
THE WHITE HART, LEWES
In south east Sussex
HORTON HOUSE
In Sussex, 7 miles west of Midhurst
THURZE HOUSE
In Sussex, an easy ride to Horton House
THE GEORGE INN
Sussex, past Midhurst, in the South Downs
LONDON
- Ranelagh Gardens
- Drury Lane
- Wyncham House, Mayfair
- Devonshire House, Mayfair

BATH
- 29 Queen Square
- The Pump Room
- The Assembly Rooms

CELEBRITY SIGHTINGS

CLIVE, CATHERINE "KITTY" (née RAFTOR)
1711 – 1785. Famed English actress and opera singer, and a close friend of Horace Walpole.

CAVENDISH, CAROLINE, DUCHESS OF DEVONSHIRE (née HOSKINS or HOSKYN)
1700 – 1777. Married the Marquis of Hartington in 1718, became Duchess in 1729. Called "Dolly" in *The Black Moth*.

CAVENDISH, WILLIAM, 3RD DUKE OF DEVONSHIRE
1698 - 1755. Ascended to the title in 1729. Statesman, soldier and one-time Lord Lieutenant of Ireland. Father of seven children and common ancestor of Charles, Prince of Wales and Lady Diana Spencer.

COVENTRY, GEORGE, 6TH EARL OF COVENTRY
1722 - 1809. Ascended to the title in 1752, the same year he married famous beauty Maria Gunning.

COVENTRY, MARIA, COUNTESS OF COVENTRY (née GUNNING)
1732 - 1760. Sister to Elizabeth, the beautiful Maria wed the Earl of Coventry in 1752. It was not a happy marriage, with the Earl taking up a mistress in the form of courtesan Kitty Fisher, much to Maria's distress. Maria, then already mother of three, died of lead poisoning at the age of 27, a "victim of cosmetics."

HAMILTON, ELIZABETH CAMPBELL, DUCHESS OF ARGYLL AND 1ST BARONESS HAMILTON OF HAMELDON (née GUNNING)
1733 - 1790. An Irish beauty of no fortune. She and her sister Maria took London by storm in 1750. Elizabeth went on to wed the Duke of Hamilton on Valentine's Day, 1972, the night they first met, in a secret wedding. The couple had three children. Following Hamilton's early death she wed the Marquis of Lorne (later Duke of Argyll), with whom she had a further five children, three of whom survived to adulthood. She was created a Baroness in her own right by George III in 1776.

HAMILTON, JAMES, 6TH DUKE OF HAMILTON
1724 - 1758. Succeeded to the title in 1743. The first husband of Elizabeth Gunning, he died at the age of 33 from a cold he caught while out hunting. Also 3rd Duke of Brandon.

DOUGLAS, WILLIAM, 4TH DUKE OF QUEENSBURY, AKA LORD MARCH
1724 - 1810. Cousin to the 3rd Duke, he had previously inherited the Earldoms of March and Ruglen from his parents. March, later fondly known as "Old Q", was famous for his love of gaming and was a great favourite of the Prince of Wales (George IV). He never married but had a daughter, Maria, who wed the Marquess of Hertford in 1798. and was the Duke's principal heir.

NASH, RICHARD "BEAU"
1674 - 1761. Though both a solider and a barrister, he is best remembered as a leader of fashion, especially in the spa town of Bath, where he served as unofficial Master of Ceremonies for almost 60 years; he served in the same post in Tunbridge Wells.

POISSON, JEANNE-ANTOINETTE, 1ST MARQUISE DE POMPADOUR
1721-1764. Mistress of King Louis XV of France and awarded the title Marquise de Pompadour. She was appointed Lady in Waiting to Louis's queen, and was among the King's most trusted advisors right up until her death.

SELWYN, GEORGE AUGUSTUS
1719 - 1791. Wit, politician, and great friend of Horace Walpole, with whom he shared a frequent correspondence. Despite his reputed intellect, he spent 44 years in the House of Commons without making a speech. An avid member of the Hellfire Club, he had a keen interest in the macabre and loved executions.

HORACE WALPOLE
1717 - 1797. Wit, gamester, epistolarian and author of *The Castle of Otranto*, generally considered to be the first Gothic novel.

~ | ~

WHAT A QUIZ!

Think you know your Heyer? These questions will test your knowledge...

1. In which year was *The Black Moth* first published?
2. By which publishing firm?
3. By what name is the Duke of Andover known in Bath?
4. In which European city did Mrs. Fanshawe meet Jack?
5. Who is Jenny?
6. In which (perhaps fictional) town is the Checquers Inn situated?
7. What is the name of Richard and Lavinia's son?
8. How did Dick cheat at cards?
9. Who does Molly O'Hara claim Jack is to her, to save him from prosecution?
10. Who is the heroine of *The Black Moth*?

ANSWERS: 1. 1921; 2. Constable; Mr. Everard; Vienna; Jack's horse; Fallowfield; John; he marked one of them with his cravat pin; her cousin; Diana Beauleigh

~ | ~

"I shall have a run of luck soon – a man can't always lose. Then I shall be able to repay you, but, of course, I shan't. It'll all go at the next table. I know!"
— *The Black Moth*, Chapter IV

"I'm afraid I always cheat," she confessed. "I had no idea it was so wicked, although Auntie gets very cross and vows she will not play with me."
— *The Black Moth*, Chapter XIV

WHAT THEY SAID

Contemporary Reviews of *The Black Moth*

The Times Literary Supplement, **London, Thursday, September 22, 1921**

This stages the eighteenth century with the usual stage business and scenery: highwaymen, duelling, gaming; and high society in London, Bath and Sussex (Horace Walpole crosses the stage for a moment). The peg on which the plot hangs is a dramatic moment when Richard Carstares, son of Lord Wyncham, cheats at cards, and his elder brother Jack, heir to the title, takes the blame, quits society and takes to the road. Jack's easy-going smiling quixotry is almost excessive; but he makes a fascinating hero of romance; and it is a well-filled story which keeps the reader pleased.

~|~

The Queenslander, **Brisbane, Saturday, June 3, 1922**

Georgette Heyer, a young authoress, has dared greatly in "The Black Moth" (Constable), for an historical novel is not the easiest thing in the world with which to hold an audience. Nevertheless, this romance of the eighteenth century will conquer by sheer merit an age which is not greatly concerned with the past. "The Black Moth" (the Duke of Andover) is such a gallant as the coffee houses of Georgian times loved to produce, a wild young rake who could win or lose his ancestral estates without a quiver. And, on the other hand, there is Lord John Carstares, convicted card cheat, an outlaw from all decent society.' The real hero of the book, however, is Andover, who, with his sinister charm and graceful selfishness, flits through the pages graciously and racily; but it is to the merry-hearted John Carstares, turned highwayman, and preying on his kind, that justice finally makes amends. The picture of Richard Carstares, the real cheat, married to the butterfly sister of Andover, forced to become banker for his brother-in-law, who knows the truth and turns it to his own advantage, is a masterly piece of character sketching.

~|~

The Springfield Sunday Republican, **Illinois, Sunday, December 25, 1921**

England in the picturesque 18th-century era of the Spectator, Henry Esmond, the stage coach and horse pistols, is made the basis of an interesting historical romance by Georgette Heyer in *The Black Moth*. in workmanship and interest it is an agreeable specimen of the historical type novel. Outstanding among the scenes portrayed in the vigorous action are the ball masque, the Pump Room at Bath, and other historical sites. Belles in crinolines and beaux in powdered wigs and silk stockings furnish a picturesqueness to the various scenes. Action is centered about "The Black Moth," a sinister figure, who wears his hair unpowdered, has other characteristic differences from the general run, and only once meets his match with a sword. There is a winsome heroine who is also the center of lively action.

~|~

SELECTED COVER GALLERY

Note: The covers of the original UK and US versions remain unknown.

Heinemann, UK
(1929)

Pan, UK
(1965)

Dutton, US
(1968)

Pan, UK
(1970)

Heinemann, UK
(1974)

Pan, UK
(1978)

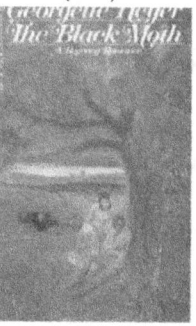
Bantam, US
(1979)

Bantam, US
(1984)

Arrow, UK
(1992)

Harlequin, Canada
(2003)

Arrow, UK
(2004)

Dodo, UK
(2008)

HQN, Canada
(2008)

Sourcebooks, US
(2009)

Dover, US
(2017)

SELECTED TRANSLATED EDITIONS

GERMAN: Zsolnay
(1971)

GERMAN: Rowohlt
(1986)

GERMAN: Verlagsunion
(1994)

DUTCH: Varrak
(2000)

ITALIAN: Harlequin
Mondadori (2005)

THE BLACK MOTH: A REMARKABLE DEBUT BY JENNIFER KLOESTER

"You do not admire our friend? Pray, do not judge him by his exterior. He may possess a beautiful mind." – *The Black Moth*, Chapter II

As might be expected of a book written in one's teens, Georgette Heyer's first novel, *The Black Moth*, is a swashbuckling tale of adventure. And yet *The Black Moth* is much more than that. Yes, it has a highwayman, swordfights, a lost earl, a wicked duke, and a damsel in distress, but there is more to this story than meets the eye.

Aged just seventeen when she made up her lively tale of romance and adventure, Georgette originally devised it as a serial story for her brother Boris, five years her junior and recovering from an illness. As she explained years later, the family had removed to Hastings on the English south coast for his convalescence and she and twelve-year-old Boris were bored, so she set about entertaining him. One can imagine Boris and perhaps even his younger brother, Frank (then aged seven), held in thrall as, chapter by chapter, Georgette told them the story of Jack Carstares, the disgraced Earl of Wyncham turned highwayman, and his enemy, "Devil" Belmanoir, Duke of Andover. The boys must have been enthusiastic for she went on writing until the story was finished. Her father, hearing some it, urged her to write it out "in her best copperplate" and submit it for publication. It was good advice, for just after her eighteenth birthday, Georgette Heyer received her first publishing contract and in September 1921, at the age of nineteen, her first novel hit the bookstands.

One hundred years later, it is still selling.

2021 will mark the centenary of *The Black Moth*, a tribute to Heyer's remarkable skill even at the tender age of seventeen. So what is it about this adolescent novel that keeps people reading? For starters it's a book that comes to life from the very first sentence:

> Clad in his customary black and silver, with raven hair unpowdered and elaborately dressed, diamonds on his fingers and in his cravat, Hugh Tracy Clare Belmanoir, Duke of Andover, sat at the escritoire in the library of his town house, writing.

So begins *The Black Moth*, the first paragraph and page introducing us to the villain of the piece: a man both attractive and sinister, Belmanoir is sneering, powerful and sardonic, and the reader is intrigued. The letter he writes and its postscript reveal both the Duke's arrogance and his disreputable past, but there is also friendship and affection for his friend, Frank Fortescue, evident in these lines. Heyer created a compelling character in a single page, and this was to become one of the hallmarks of her novels.

From the Prologue featuring 'Devil" Belmanoir, Heyer dives straight into the main story – that of Jack Carstares, Earl of Wyncham, highwayman and sometime aristocrat in the guise of the very debonair Sir Anthony Ferndale. Jack is a classic hero, genial, handsome and, in what was to become true Heyer style, a fastidious and tasteful dresser. He is also good with horses, handy with his sword and fists, and definitely a man of honour. It is this last upon which the plot of the novel depends, for Jack has given up his earldom and spent the past six years abroad, cruelly separated from his family and friends, and with his reputation in tatters because he has confessed to… shock! horror!... cheating at cards. To the modern reader this may seem a ludicrous reason to give up one's life, but in Heyer's world and in the world of eighteenth-century England, gambling debts were considered "debts of honour"; to be deemed a cheat was akin to being a traitor. Of course, our Jack is no cheat but a loyal loving brother. as we discover in the very first chapter. The second chapter reveals him to be kind, generous and fond of a joke. The dialogue flows, Heyer's love of debonair, finely-dressed men with decided taste is established and the stage is set.

It is worth remembering that *The Black Moth* was written as a serial. Of course, we cannot know how much of the story Heyer wrote in advance of each day's telling or whether one of more chapters comprised an episode but the chapter headings do suggest that she told her brothers one chapter at a time and it took her eight chapters to introduce her audience to all the main players in her melodrama. Within each episode, however, there is vibrant dialogue, excellent characterisation and several intriguing sub-plots. Though the story is young in many ways and typical of its time and genre, Heyer's skill – even in her teen years – is undeniable, and there is a depth of emotion in Jack, Lady Lavinia, Richard and even in his Grace of Andover, that is surprising. The section in Chapter VIII, "The Biter Bit", where she reveals some of Jack's innermost thoughts, touching on "all the old misery and impotent resentment", is surprisingly moving. Heyer's characters are flesh-and-blood and for all its fun and frivolity, there are moments of real pathos in *The Black Moth*.

While it has been suggested, given her tender years, that Georgette's father may have had a hand in the writing of *The Black Moth*, there is no evidence of this. Certainly, her father, George Heyer, read her manuscripts, just as she read his, but his writing style – as seen in his poems and short prose pieces – are rather different from his daughter's. He certainly checked his daughter's syntax, grammar, French phraseology and very likely helped in the creation of some of the poems in her novels (most notably in *The Transformation of Philip Jettan*, aka *Powder and Patch*), but the style and prose of all of the books that she wrote after her father's sudden death in 1925 show clearly that from the very first Georgette Heyer's novels were very much her own.

The Black Moth is not without its flaws, there are stereotypes here and unlikely coincidences and high romance, but as a first novel and as a portent of things to come, it is a worthy beginning and well-deserving of its centenary in print.

— *Jennifer Kloester*

~ | ~

"I do not like your name, sir," she answered.
  "There was no thought of pleasing you when I was christened," he quoted lazily.
  "Hardly, sir," she said. "You might be my father."
— *The Black Moth*, Chapter XXV

Bit by bit my lord discovered that he was very much in love with Diana. At first his heart gave a great bound, and then seemed to stop with a sickening thud.
— *The Black Moth*, Chapter XIV

~ | ~

HAPPY 100TH BIRTHDAY TO *THE BLACK MOTH* IN SEPTEMBER, 2021!

NONPAREIL

International Heyer Society Circular #2, August 2020

FROM THE PATRONESSES

Welcome to the second edition of *Nonpareil*, and the second month of the International Heyer Society!

With our numbers having increased pleasingly in such a very short space of time, we are so excited to share with you all some deep thoughts on one of Georgette Heyer's lesser known (some would say, deservedly) works, *The Great Roxhythe*, a historical novel set in the era of Charles II, and published when she was just twenty years of age.

~|~

The King was naturally above reproach. Equally above reproach was Roxhythe.
— *The Great Roxhythe*, Book II, Chapter I

"Nothing is so alluring as the 'ought not', beloved."
— *The Great Roxhythe*, Book II, Chapter V

~|~

THE GREAT ROXHYTHE

Georgette Heyer's second novel was quite unlike her first. Where *The Black Moth* was a high romance filled with adventure, *The Great Roxhythe* was a much more serious book about Charles II's court and the many political intrigues of the day. It was also Heyer's first tragedy and her first novel to eschew a central romance. Published by Hutchinson in 1922, it is a well-written book which reveals something of the young Georgette's early ambitions as a writer. Her first novel had been devised to entertain her convalescent younger brother; this second book was an attempt at more 'serious' historical fiction. While there is no denying that  *The Great Roxhythe* was a remarkable achievement for a nineteen-year-old author, it was not where Heyer's forte lay. Fortunately, the book helped to lay the groundwork for the novels to come and it also revealed her undeniable ability to put flesh on the bones of history for her depiction of the post-Restoration world, its historical realities and political machinations is convincing.

In its day, *The Great Roxhythe* was a success. In 1929, Heinemann bought the rights to the novel from Hutchinson and by 1935 the book had enjoyed six printings in at least three different editions. But Georgette Heyer grew to loathe it; years later she described as a 'very jejune work' and 'just the kind of book you'd expect from an over-ambitious teenager' and by 1940 she had firmly suppressed it.

— *Jennifer Kloester*

~|~

THE CHARACTERS

DAVID, MARQUIS OF ROXHYTHE
A firm favourite of Charles II, the incisive Roxhythe's years of espionage and intrigue on behalf of His Majesty are little suspected by those who see him as nothing more than a handsome courtier of great wit and charm.

CHRISTOPHER DART
Roxhythe's most ardent adherent, the young and idealistic patriot spends years defending his lord, only to discover how wrong he was. Heartbroken, he is never the same.

LADY FRANCES "FANNY" MONTGOMERY
Cousin to Roxhythe, a clever and bewitching beauty, and perhaps the only person, aside from the King, to begin to comprehend Roxhythe's true depth of cunning. Glad she didn't marry him.

MILLICENT, LADY CREWE
A young and beautiful newlywed with whose affections Roxhythe trifles, for some reason.

SIR HENRY CREWE
Her husband, who takes understandable — if unpleasantly violent — exception.

SIR JASPER MONTGOMERY
Fanny's stalwart, if unimaginative, husband.

RODERICK DART
Christopher's prim brother, ostensibly in the service of Holland's parliament but secretly a huge William of Orange stan.

MYNHEER DE STAAL
A Dutch apothecary and big fan of Roxhythe.

EDWARD MILWARD
A French spy, easily fooled by the Marquis.

DUPONT
Another French spy, much better at his job.

SYDNEY HARCOURT
An old friend of Christopher's; political functionary; dubious of Roxhythe and shows it, making his old friend Chris quite angry.

FORTESCUE
Can't handle his liquor.

CHARLOTTE D'ALMOND
A virago, yet fascinating.

JOHN
Roxhythe's devoted servant.

MR. BURNEST
A physician.

~ | ~

> "You did your best to break my heart—and now you reveal yourself to me — callous, ruthless! It—hurts damnably, my lord."
> — *The Great Roxhythe*, Book IV, Chapter V

> "In a good cause you were invaluable. But you are inconsistent. Like the wind, you veer first one way in your policy, and then the other."
> — *The Great Roxhythe*, Book IV, Chapter III

~ | ~

THE LOCATIONS

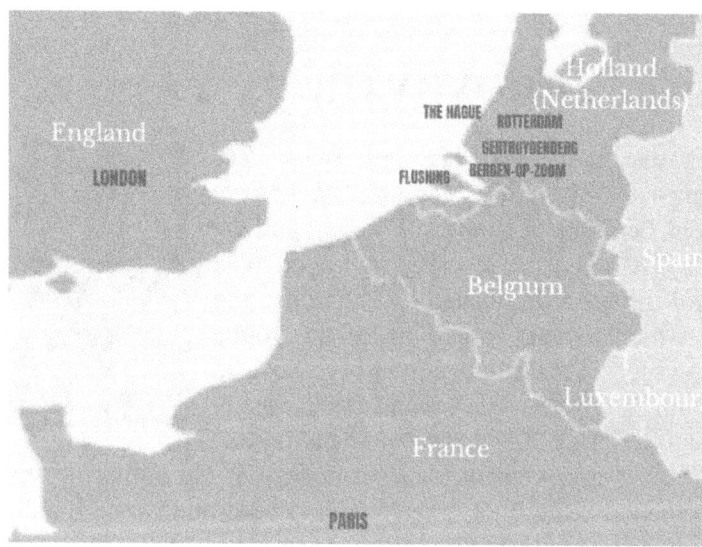

LONDON
- Bevan House, The Strand
- 7 Milford Lane
- 8, Cheapside
- Palace of Whitehall

BEVAN COURT
Unknown location somewhere in England

PARIS
- The Louvre

FLUSHING (NOW VLISSINGEN)
- The Sceptre Inn

BERGEN-OP-ZOOM

GERTRUYDENBERG

ROTTERDAM
- 19, Prinsen Straat

THE HAGUE
- The Three Fishers Inn
- Poisson d'Or Inn
- Noordeinde Palace
- Scheveningen

~ | ~

> "I see, sir, that you know my name. May I not have the honour of yours?"
> His lordship's brows rose.
> "I am Roxhythe," he said, with faint surprise. The naïve egotism passed over Christopher's head. He stood transfixed in an amazement that plainly showed itself on his face. He recovered, and bowed again.
> "I am indeed honoured," he said.
> Roxhythe's lip quivered.
> "On the contrary," he replied. "The honour is mine."
> — *The Great Roxhythe*, Book I, Chapter I

CELEBRITY SIGHTINGS

ARUNDELL, HENRY, 3RD BARON ARUNDEL OF WARDOUR
(1607 - 1694) Messenger to Charles II, he was implicated in the so-called Popish Plot and sent to the Tower, though was never tried. He became a Privy Councillor under James II.

ASHLEY COOPER, ANTHONY, 1ST EARL OF SHAFTESBURY
(1621 – 1683) A powerful political figure, he was among the so-called Cabal Ministry and was at frequent odds with Charles II. He was especially opposed to the concept of absolute rule, eventually being arrested for high treason for his support of the Exclusion Bill, which would have prevented Catholics from taking the throne.

BARILLON D'AMONCOURT, PAUL, MARQUIS DE BRANGES
(1630–1691) French Ambassador to England from 1667-1688, he was treated with great civility by Charles II and James II, and is considered one of the great diplomats of the era. During the later years of Charles II's reign, Barillon was employed as an intermediary between Louis XIV and various disgruntled English statesmen and courtiers. Nevertheless, he was at Charles II's bedside when he died, having been permitted to send a secret message of his illness to Louis, and stayed as an honoured guest in England until exiled by William III in 1688.

BEALINGS, SIR RICHARD
(1622 – 1716) Irish courtier who was Knight secretary to Queen Catherine, and signatory to the Secret Treaty of Dover.

BENNET, HENRY, 1ST EARL OF ARLINGTON
(1618 – 1685) A long-time supporter of Charles II, for a time he was the King's prime favourite, but he was eventually ousted from all influence by his more successful rivals.

BENTINCK, WILLIAM, 1ST EARL OF PORTLAND
(1649 – 1709) Friend and trusted messenger of William III, he was also a solider, diplomat, and man of great jealousy.

CATHERINE OF BRAGANZA
(1638 - 1705) Princess Caterina of Portugal was wed to Charles II in 1662. Her lot was not a happy one, and on Charles's deathbed she sent a note asking he pardon her if she had "offended" him. (More below.)

CHARLES II OF ENGLAND
(1630 – 1685) Son of the ousted Charles I, he fled England for France in 1651 and spent seven years in exile. Returned to the throne during the Restoration, his reign became a byword for decadence, and he is now mostly remembered for his great personal charm, multiple mistresses (by whom he had 21 children), secret dealings, and love of spaniels.

CHIFFINCH, WILLIAM
(1602 – 1691) Charles II's Page of the Bedchamber and Keeper of his Private Closet. Yes, those are real titles.

CLIFFORD, THOMAS, 1ST BARON CHUDLEIGH
(1630 – 1673) Distinguished naval officer, member of the Cabal and prominent Catholic who died by his own hand after resigning as Lord High Treasurer.

COLBERT, CHARLES, MARQUIS DE CROISSY
(1625 – 1696) French ambassador to England during the negotiations for the Secret Treaty of Dover.

COVENTRY, SIR WILLIAM
(1628 – 1686) Naval administrator, Privy Councillor and opponent to Catholic rule of England.

DE BEAUVILLIERS, FRANCOIS-HONORAT, 1ST DUKE DE SAINT-AIGNAN
(1607 – 1687) Soldier, administrator, writer and, apparently, great friend of the Marquis of Roxhythe.

DE BOURBON, HENRI JULES, PRINCE DE CONDÉ
(1643 – 1709) A French general and domestic abuser diagnosed with clinical lycanthropy in his declining years. Great-Grandfather of the one who fell for Léonie.

DE COURCILLON, PHILIPPE, MARQUIS DE DANGEAU
(1638 – 1720) A soldier, diplomat and diarist, whose "insipid" decades of entries nevertheless contain much insight and detail about the France of Louis XIV.

DE GRAMADN, GUY-ARMAND, COMTE DE GUICHE
(1637 - 1673) Famous for his skill on the battlefield and for his affair with Philippe de France, brother to Louis XIV.

DE KÉROUAILLE, LOUISE, DUCHESS OF PORTSMOUTH
(1630–1691) French-born mistress of Charles II who was supported in lavish style, worked hard for France, and maintained a strong friendship with Queen Catherine, but was much hated by the people of England. Especially Nell Gwyn.

DE LA TOUR, D'AUVERNGE, HENRI, VICOMTE DE TURENNE
(11611 – 1675) A French Marshal General, considered one of the greatest military commanders in modern history. Upon his death in battle in 1675, he was mourned throughout France, and as he was considered a "man of people" his tomb was held inviolate in the Revolution.

DE ROCHECHOUART, FRANCOISE-ATHÉNAÏS, MARQUISE DE MONTESPAN
(1640 - 1707) Maîtresse-en-titre (Chief Royal Mistress) to Louis XIV, with whom she had seven children, many of whom were legitimized and married into European royalty. Suspected of poisoning a rival, she fell from favour in 1681.

DE RUYTER, MICHIEL ADRIAENZOON
(1607 – 1676) Dutch Admiral much beloved of his subordinates and country, was known as bestevaêr (grandfather), and is still revered as a folk hero.

DE WITT, JOHAN
(1625 – 1672) Rising to the title of Grand Pensionary of Holland, De Witt opposed royal rule and led Holland into a period of profound economic growth during his decades in office, while keeping heir-to-the-throne William Nassau, Prince of Orange, imprisoned. He, alongside his brother Cornelius, was lynched by an angry mob (possibly incited by William) following the Franco-English invasion of 1672.

DIGBY, GEORGE, 2ND EARL OF BRISTOL
(1612 - 1677) Orator, statesman and supporter of Charles II famous for his instability and frequently questionable advice.

FERGUSON, ROBERT
(1637 - 1714) Known as "the Plotter," he was a Scottish presbyterian minister who took an active part in the Rye House Plot to assassinate Charles II and his brother James.

GREY, FORD, LORD GREY OF WARKE, 1ST EARL OF TANKERVILLE
(1655 – 1701) A strong supporter of the Duke of Monmouth, he was involved in the Rye House Plot but escaped the Tower of London, fleeing to France with his wife's sister, her husband in tow. He was a leader of the Monmouth Rebellion was arrested on multiple charges, but turned informer and was restored to his dignities. William III made him a Privy Councillor and Lord Justice of the Realm.

GWYN, ELEANOR "NELL"
(1650 – 1687) Probably the most famous of Charles II's many mistresses, she was an actress dubbed "pretty, witty Nell" by Samuel Pepys, and was often at odds with some of her high-born... colleagues at Court. She had two sons with Charles, and was granted a royal pension under James II.

HOLLES, DENZIL, 1ST BARON HOLLES
(1599 - 1680) Helped spark the English Civil War by attempting to arrest Charles I. His influence survived under both Cromwell and Charles II; he plotted against the latter with envoys of Louis XIV.

HOWARD, WILLIAM, 1ST VISCOUNT STAFFORD
(1614 - 1680) A Royalist and scientist, he was falsely implicated in the Popish Plot and executed, despite his innocence being well-known. Beatified by the Pope in 1929.

HUDDLESTON, FATHER JOHN
(1608 - 1698) A Catholic priest and monk who aided Charles II in his escape from Cromwell and took the King's confession at his death.

HUTCHINS, SIR GEORGE
(d. 1705) Barrister, Serjeant-at-Law to James II, King's Serjeant to William III.

HYDE, HENRY 2ND EARL OF CLARENDON
(1638 – 1709) Uncle of Mary II and Queen Anne, brother-in-law to James II, one-time private secretary to Queen Catherine and Lord Privy Seal from 1685 until he fell from favour in 1687. He was not a supporter of William III and spent some time in the Tower as a result.

JAMES II OF ENGLAND
(1633 – 1701) Brother to Charles II and noted commander at sea, the Duke of York came to the throne in 1685, but was removed in 1688 – mostly due to his avowed Catholicism. Several attempts to reclaim his throne failed, and he spent the remainder of his life in exile in France under the protection of his cousin Louis XIV.

KILLIGREW, SIR THOMAS
(1612 – 1683) Dramatist, producer and noted wit, he was page to Charles I and Master of Revels to Charles II.

LOUIS XIV OF FRANCE
(1638 – 1715) Called Louis the Great and the Sun King, he reigned for 72 years, coming to the throne at the age of four. Under his rule France became a great military power, but he is mostly remembered for the opulence of his Court, the unfairness of his taxation, and, like his contemporary Charles II, for his plentiful mistresses.

MAITLAND, JOHN, 1ST DUKE OF LAUDERDALE
(1616 – 1682) Scottish peer, leader with the

Cabal Ministry, and strong favourite of both Charles II and James II, his influence was often challenged but rarely shaken.

MARY II OF ENGLAND
(1662 - 1694) Wed to the Prince of Orange at age sixteen, the pair took the throne after Mary's father James II was removed from it in 1689. She died of smallpox at the age of 32, reportedly leaving her husband devastated.

PALMER, BARBARA, 1ST DUCHESS OF CLEVELAND
(1640 – 1709) aka Lady Castlemaine. Acclaimed beauty and mistress to Charles II, mother to five of his children, all acknowledged and ennobled, despite their illegitimacy. So great was her influence that she was known as "the Uncrowned Queen."

OATES, TITUS
(1649 – 1705) A priest and conman, not in that order, he, with Israel Tonge, fabricated the "Popish Plot," alleging a Catholic conspiracy to assassinate Charles II. This led to years of investigation and the execution of at least fifteen before the so-called plot was disproved. Oates's various punishments included an enormous fine, imprisonment, and several kinds of torture. After three years he was pardoned and awarded a pension by William III.

RUMBOLD, RICHARD
(1622 - 1685) A Cromwell loyalist who took a part – among many others – in the 1683 Rye House Plot. He escaped prosecution but was executed for his part in a later attempt on James II.

RUMSEY, COLONEL JOHN
(1601 – circa 1686) Another conspirator in the Rye House Plot, as well as in the Monmouth Rebellion.

RUSSELL, WILLIAM, LORD RUSSELL
(1639 – 1683) A leading member of the Country Party, he was beheaded for treason by Charles II.

SACKVILLE, CHARLES, 1ST EARL OF DORSET
(1643 – 1706) Known also as Lord Buckhurst, he was a poet, courtier and dramatist known for his wit and rapaciousness.

SAVILE, GEORGE, 1ST MARQUESS HALIFAX
(1633 - 1695) Privy Councillor, Fellow of the Royal Society and Popish Plot dupe kicked out by James II.

SCOTT, JAMES, DUKE OF MONMOUTH
(1649 – 1685) Eldest son of Charles II, at the age of fourteen he was wed to twelve-year-old heiress Anne Scott, and took her name. He led a rebellion against his uncle James II, despite is illegitimacy, and was beheaded for treason.

SEDLEY, SIR CHARLES
(1639 – 1701) Dramatist, politician, spendthrift and noted wit.

SPENCER, ROBERT, 2ND EARL OF SUNDERLAND
(1641 - 1702) A believer in absolute monarchy, he was an upright, forthright and somewhat dull figure who was hated by James II but loved by William III.

STEWART, FRANCES TERESA, DUCHESS OF RICHMOND AND LENNOX
(1647 – 1702) A great beauty mostly famed for refusing to become Charles II's mistress, leading him to consider divorcing his Queen.

STUART, HENRIETTE, DUCHESSE D'ORLEANS
(1644 – 1670) Known as "Madame", she was sister to Charles II (and James II), and wife to Louis XIV's brother. Clever and charming and with a gift for diplomacy, her romantic intrigues were often marred by her husband's interest in the same men.

TEMPLE, SIR WILLIAM
(1628 – 1699) Diplomat, essayist and architect of the marriage between William and Mary.

TRENCHARD, SIR JOHN
(1649 - 1695) Involved in the Rye House Plot but never arrested, he later became a statesman under William III.

TUBERVILLE, EDWARD
(1648 – 1681) Welsh soldier who falsely testified against Lord Stafford of a plot to assassinate Charles II, leading to Stafford's execution.

VILLIERS, GEORGE, 2ND DUKE OF BUCKINGHAM
(1628 – 1687) Brought up with Charles I, close ally of Charles II, member of the Cabal Ministry and all-around schemer brought down by his own ambition.

WHARTON, THOMAS, 1ST MARQUESS OF WHARTON
(1648 – 1715) Known for his charm, debauchery and political genius, he was a long-serving member of Parliament imprisoned in the Tower by Charles II, an enemy of James II, an ally of William III, disliked by Anne and favoured by George I.

WILLIAM OF ORANGE
(1650 - 1702) Dutch royal, nephew of Charles II and able military commander, he spent his early years under house arrest by the Dutch Parliament, but took power in 1672. He was installed as William III of England, alongside his wife Mary II, after the removal of his Catholic father-in-law James II in 1688. Puritanical and avowedly Protestant, he waged war on Catholicism in Ireland and is remembered there as either a villain or a hero, depending upon whom you ask.

~ | ~

WHAT A QUIZ!

Think you know your Heyer? These questions will test your knowledge...

1. In which year was *The Great Roxhythe* first published?
2. Which English monarchs appear as characters?
3. By what nickname is the Duchess d'Orleans known?
4. Where did Roxhythe first meet William of Orange?
5. Who is Christopher Dart's brother?
6. Who was King of France during Charles II's reign?
7. In how many Georgette Heyer novels does Charles II appear?
8. How many children did Charles II have?
9. What is the name of the 1683 plot to assassinate Charles II and his brother James, Duke of York?
10. What is the Marquis of Roxhythe's surname?

ANSWERS: 1. 1922 (US, 1923); 2. Charles II, James II, William III, Mary II; Madame; The Hague; Roderick Dart; Louis XIV; 2: *The Great Roxhythe* and *Royal Escape*; 21; The Rye House Plot; We don't know! But we can speculate it is "Bevan" as that is the name of both his town and country houses.

WHAT THEY SAID

Contemporary Reviews of *The Great Roxhythe*

The New York Times Book Review, **June 24, 1923**

The colorful period of the English Restoration, brilliant, witty, cynical, amusing and immoral, taking its tone from the witty, cynical and charming King who stands in its forefront, has always possessed a fascination for writers of romances. And a good deal of fascination, too, for the reader, who gets the thrill of the so-called Popish plot, of the intrigues and the perils, the turmoil over the Exclusion bill, vicariously, and without any of the dangers that beset the men and women of the time. But if the men of the time make an interesting group, a group composed for the most part of strongly contrasted and no less strongly emphasized individualities, it is the women gathered about the King, from the unhappy Queen herself to that frolicsome baggage Nell Gwynne, on whom the attention of the romances is usually fixed.

It is here that Georgette Heyer's novel breaks sharply with tradition. For, though the beautiful Henriette d'Angleterre, Duchesse d'Orléans, appears several times, though the Duchess of Portsmouth, Lady Castlemaine, and the Duchess of Cleveland form part of the story's background, it is principally a tale of men, and the deep love and friendship of men for one another. The strongest emotion in the life of Christopher Dart, the young, ingenuous, idealistic patriot who became secretary to the Most Noble the Marquis of Roxhythe, was his adoring love for the man who was his lord and master, the man he trusted absolutely, against whom he was warned more than once, but of whom he would believe no evil until, and to his lasting grief, that evil was proved, and proved up to the hilt. And as the strongest emotion in Christopher's life was his affection for Roxhythe so the motive power in Roxhythe's life, the feeling to which he sacrificed everything and everyone, Christopher included, was the bond which held him to the King. As his cousin and friend, Lady Fanny Montgomery, once told him, he had sacrificed "truth, honour, patriotism for man"; for the King's sake he had lied and intrigued and betrayed until no one else trusted him.

Beginning in 1668, when Charles had been on the throne for only a few years, the novel closes not long after the accession of the stupid and ill-fated James. And while it gives an interesting picture of the life of the time as seen and lived by one who was the favorite and constant companion of Charles II, it suffers somewhat from having too large a canvas, and from a certain monotony in the telling. My lord's exploit in Holland, his very interesting interview with that Prince of Orange who was one day to become King of England, form one episode. Then comes the Treaty of Dover, when Charles sold his country to France. followed by the intrigues regarding the succession, and the plot to exclude James from the throne. Charles's triumph and his death. The effect of climax, of an accumulative building up is lacking, and this lack injures the drama of it all. Then, too, the book is very much too long: there is a great deal of repetition, many incidents and conversations which do little to develop character, while of story there is almost none. For the book is primarily the study of a single complex character, the character of "The Great Roxhythe."

To the men and women surrounding him he was an enigma; even the "little master" he loved so dearly did not always understand him, although the clue lay in his devotion to that same master. Brilliantly clever, extremely able, cynical. graceful and gracious, kindly and cruel, cool, self-possessed at all times, courageous, daring, clear-sighted and clear-headed, the reader is made to feel more than a little of the fascination to which young Christopher so utterly succumbed. There are in the book a number of clever sketches of men and women; most notable, perhaps, the portrait of the Prince of Orange. A colorful and interesting account of a colorful and interesting period is this which Georgette Heyer presents to us under the name of the man who to a very great extent personifies it, the man who is here represented as the power behind the throne. David. Marquis of Roxhythe, whose one aim and desire in life was to do the King's pleasure."

The Scotsman, **Edinburgh, January 15, 1923**

In preparation for writing her romance of the seventeenth century, *The Great Roxhythe*, Miss Georgette Heyer must have studied to good purpose the annals of the period of Charles II. The story follows, with a considerable measure of precision, the intrigues and plots, at Court and abroad, that take up so large a part of the reign of the "Merry Monarch," who, with his brother James, his son the Duke of Monmouth, and other leading figures of the Court, comes prominently on the scene, as does also William, Prince of Orange, and several of the beauties of Charles's reign. It cannot be said that the Marquis of Roxhythe is readily identified with any of the notables of the time. Like the Royal master whom he serves all too well, he is devoid of scruple or principle, at least where Charles's interests are concerned; and like the King, also, all his charm does not save him from earning contempt. Revelation of his real character and conduct causes cruel pain to his secretary, Christopher Dart, who is devotedly attached to him, and whose alienation brings to the "Great Roxhythe" the sharpest twinge of regret and remorse that he is capable of feeling.

~ | ~

The Spectator, **London, January 27, 1923**

This is a very ambitious historical romance, covering the later years of Charles II's reign from the Secret Treaty of Dover to the Exclusion Bill, the Rye House Plot and the King's death. The author has taken great pains to present in Roxhythe a man of power and charm who deliberately subordinates his better feelings to his passionate devotion to the King. His young secretary, who has a profound regard for Roxhythe, finds that there is a point at which patriotism, as he conceives it, must outweigh personal affection, but for Roxhythe there is no such limit. As a character-study Roxhythe deserves praise, but readers who are not fully versed in the politics of Charles II's time may find that the story drags. The author's reading of history is plausible enough and the details are sufficiently accurate. But she ought to know that people in the later Stuart age did not write their letters on parchment, which was reserved, then as now, for legal documents of importance.

~ | ~

SELECTED COVER GALLERY

Note: No known translated versions exist.

Hutchinson, UK (1922)

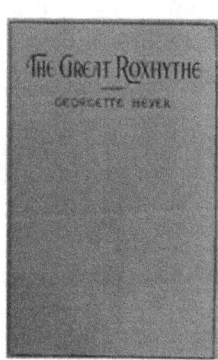

Small Maynard, US (1923)

Heinemann, UK (1929)

Heinemann, UK (1951)

Amereon House, US (2006)

ROXHYTHE SYNDROME BY RACHEL HYLAND

"'Tis always the same. You may be never so angry with him when he is absent, but the moment you see him—pouf! The anger is gone!"
— *The Great Roxhythe*, Book II, Chapter VII

Stockholm Syndrome has, courtesy mostly of pop culture, become one of the better known among all psychological phenomena. Defined as "Feelings of trust or affection felt in many cases of kidnapping or hostage-taking by a victim towards a captor," it is a condition that is little understood and, in fact, has never been officially established in the halls of academia — even the name by which we know it comes from secular sources, as it was coined by the media following a bank robbery in the titular Swedish city in 1973 — and yet we all know it when we (think we) see it, or feel it, and I swear that I am experiencing it even as I write this.

Because I think I love The *Great Roxhythe* now.

To anyone who has read Georgette Heyer's second novel, a somewhat dense history of post-Restoration England as seen through the eyes of her singular addition to its annals, the suave and ruthless David, the Most Noble the Marquis of Roxhythe, coming on the back of her well-known and beloved Georgian and Regency romances, or even her more successful historical attempts, like *Simon the Coldheart* and *Royal Escape*, this claim might seem outrageous. Roxhythe is, in the main, not considered great at all, and is among the least favourite of most aficionados—even including Heyer herself.

Certainly, my early thoughts on this novel were less than positive. In an essay in *Heyer Society*, I break it down thoroughly for the reader, and state baldly that had it been my first Heyer, I probably wouldn't have read a second. I talk of it showing evidence of Heyer's "nascent genius" and commend its scholarship (of which, more anon), but it is clear that I found it something of a disappointment. To wit: "Heyer's dab hand at the history stuff is certainly on display here, and is impressive as hell, except that it's also a little... well... dry. It's almost like this novel started out as a high school essay on the power struggle between the Catholics and the Protestants in Stuart-era England, or even of the political machinations undertaken by Charles II, or even of Charles II and his many mistresses..."

And you know what? Maybe it did. But having read this book now with the most painstaking attention I have paid to anything except perhaps the intricacies of the Star Trek universe, I have to recant my suggestion that it is in any way "dry." Because for all that I still believe that "the reader is given perhaps a shade too much credit for personal knowledge of some fairly obscure historical events," and it did indeed have me "awash in a sea of bubbling confusion for pretty much the duration," the fact is, now that I have taken the time to thoroughly research each incident and pretty much every personage mentioned throughout this... you know what? I'm gonna say it... triumph of a novel, I have a whole new appreciation for it. As you can tell.

Such is the true genius of Heyer.

With each reread, something new is revealed.

And mostly what was revealed to me in this one is just how incredible it is.

Let's talk a little about the scholarship on display here, because for a start, she wrote this when she was nineteen, and also, she wrote it without the aid of, as for example, the internet. When she was casually introducing Mr. Chiffinch, Charles II's confidential page, or throwing off a reference to Sir George Hutchins, a barrister of the time, she had to know about these people, that these people were there, and what their deal was. She had to read histories much denser than this one, no doubt, as well as diaries and Court documents and letters and more than just the Encyclopaedia, to get all of this detail correct. I'm not saying it is a flawless history (according to current knowledge, which is ALL THE KNOWLEDGE, a few of her dates, when it comes to certain people, seem a little out of whack), but by and large, she nailed this fictionalized account of the time in simply stunning fashion. I cannot state that enough.

Moreover, the central figure of the narrative, Roxhythe himself, is a far more interesting creature than I previously gave him credit for, in earlier readings of this novel. Going back to my essay, I called him "... rather too cold-blooded, too unlikeable, to be a true hero for us here." But, upon reflection, I just don't think that's true.

It is only that he is not a true romantic hero.

But that's okay. He isn't supposed to be.

He's supposed to be a schemer, a charmer, the power behind the throne. He's supposed to dupe and deceive and disguise, to do anything he must do to make Charles his life easier. (Wow, I'm even talking like Roxhythe now.) He's Heyer's Sir Percy Blakeney, but his cause is his King, not French aristos in need of sanctuary. And Christopher Dart, his earnest, kind-hearted and – it has to be said – gullible secretary is this book's Marguerite.

Indeed, the biggest stumbling block most readers have with Roxhythe is the lack of a central romance. There are affairs and dalliances (my lord is quite the cad), lots of flowery compliments poured into shell-like ears, and a lot of very open, very vocal and physical affection shown between men, especially between man and master. Roxhythe's secretary Chris – oh, dear, sweet, disillusioned Chris – is forever kissing Roxhythe's hand, for example. And Roxhythe is very ardent in his attentions to His Majesty, Charles II. Their words to, and about, each other are nothing short of lover-like. And yet there is no couple here to cheer for (if only!), and most assuredly no happy ending, this being one of Heyer's few tragedies. That can be jarring, when you see the name "Georgette Heyer" on the cover.

And I think that is why this is book is so generally unpopular.

But the fact is, there's nothing at all wrong with the book. For any fan of its genre, it is undoubtedly a fine piece of work. At least as fine as The Conqueror, anyway. It's just that the Heyerness we were expecting isn't quite there, and so we find ourselves left puzzled, and yes, disappointed, by its distinctiveness in her canon.

I say, instead, we should be proud.

Proud that she should have produced something so profoundly impressive at such a young age. Proud that she experimented with styles, with characters and with different time periods for all of her life. And proud that we all have Heyer Syndrome. I, for one, am grateful for it.

— *Rachel Hyland*

~ | ~

"I am very glad I did not marry you," she told him.
"So am I," said my lord. "We should have quarrelled. 'Tis ever the way when both have wit. I suppose you never quarrel with Jasper?"
— *The Great Roxhythe*, Book II, Chapter III

"...since I have been with—Roxhythe—he has had all my love. He has it still. There will never be another in his place. I'm a weak fool—but—oh, Lady Frances, I want him so much!"
— *The Great Roxhythe*, Book IV, Chapter VI

~ | ~

"I tell you, he is a devil. You might be bound to him with chains, and he would give you the slip. He is not a man. He is a devil."
— *The Great Roxhythe*, Book I, Chapter VII

"You cannot hope to understand the workings of the game; one must be bred up in it. You may not condemn that which you do not understand."
— *The Great Roxhythe*, Book II, Chapter IX

NONPAREIL

International Heyer Society Circular #3, September 2020

FROM THE PATRONESSES

It's our third edition, and here we come to one of Heyer's popular Georgian outings, originally published as *The Transformation of Philip Jettan*, but now more commonly known by its 1930 reissued title, *Powder and Patch*. Don't miss the Great Debate on the relative merits of our heroine Cleone, the breakdown of the characters and locations, or the trivia quiz!

> With Philip's departure had come a void which only could be filled by Philip's return.
> — *Powder and Patch*, Chapter V

> "James, sit down! You should know by now the sight of anyone on their feet fatigues me, silly boy!"
> — *Powder and Patch*, Chapter XIV

THE TRANSFORMATION OF PHILIP JETTAN

I HAVE often wondered why Georgette Heyer wrote her third novel under a pseudonym. *The Transformation of Philip Jettan* by "Stella Martin" was first published by Mills & Boon in April 1923. At the time, Heyer was contracted to Hutchinson; the previous year they had published her first serious historical work, *The Great Roxhythe*, about the court of Charles II, and were to publish her first contemporary novel, *Instead of the Thorn* in November. A lighthearted, frivolous "bubble" of a novel could not have been more different. In 1923 Georgette still had not settled on one specific genre – that would take another twenty years – but there was nothing in *Philip Jettan* of which to be ashamed. She might have thought that Hutchinson would not wish to publish such an amusing and carefree story between two more serious and sedate ones. It might also be that being under contract for just two novels, Heyer would not have wanted to complicate matters or possibly infringe the terms by publishing a book under her own name with a different publisher.

Another reason might have been to do with her father. I have sometimes wondered if perhaps George Heyer had more of a hand in *Philip Jettan* than Georgette felt able to acknowledge publicly and so the nom de plume became a useful cover for a joint effort. Although that didn't stop her from allowing Heinemann to republish the novel under her own name in 1930, under its new title of *Powder and Patch*. Her father was dead by then, of course, so perhaps that made a difference. I do think it very likely that her father wrote the poetry in *Philip Jettan*, or at the very least helped to write it. George was a talented amateur poet with a love of the rondeau, the ballade and the villanelle and was an idiomatic French speaker. His influence on Georgette's third novel seems unmistakeable. It is also true that Georgette Heyer wrote *The Transformation of Philip Jettan* in just three weeks – the fastest of all her novels. Was this something that concerned her? Did it perhaps affect her perception of the novel? Was it something that she had "thrown off" and therefore not worth submitting to her current publisher? Instead she gave the book to Mills & Boon. Not yet the genre-specific publisher they would become in the late 1930s, in 1923 Mills & Boon were a medium-sized general publisher with a wide-ranging list of fiction and non-fiction books. Having written this "elegant trifle" did Georgette simply decide that she might as well submit the manuscript somewhere but not under her real name? Perhaps it was a test, to see if her writing really was good enough to win publication as an unknown author. It is unclear whether Mills & Boon knew before 1930, when Heinemann republished the book, that their "debut author", Stella Martin was bestselling novelist Georgette Heyer.

I suspect we will never really know why she wrote this one novel under a pseudonym but it's fun to speculate and no matter the reason we'll always have *The Transformation of Philip Jettan* to entertain us.

— *Jennifer Kloester*

THE CHARACTERS

PHILIP JETTAN
A bluff, manly and countrified gentleman who wants nothing more than to marry the girl next door and settle down. Instead, he finds himself compelled to go to Paris and get a makeover. A *revenge* makeover.

SIR MAURICE JETTAN
Philip's father, a man of fashion who longs to see his uncouth son learn the ways of the Polite World.

MARIA, LADY JETTAN
Maurice's deceased wife, Philip's mother.

THOMAS JETTAN
Philip's kindly uncle, who happily abets him in all of his plans. Hopelessly in love with Lady Sally Malmerstoke.

SIR THOMAS JETTAN
Father to Maurice and Tom, it was he who built the grand country manor that came to be known as Jettan's Pride.

CLEONE CHARTERIS
Beautiful and indulged, Cleone loves Philip but wishes he could be courtlier and more refined, and cared more for his clothes. Cleone should be careful what she wishes for.

MADAME CHARTERIS
Cleone's placid mother.

MR. CHARTERIS
Her genial father, on good terms with Sir Maurice.

JAMES WINTON
A childhood friend of Philip and Cleone's, now with an enormous crush on the latter.

JENNIFER WINTON
James's sister, a sweet and naive newcomer to London, in some awe of Cleone, and Philip.

LADY SARAH "SALLY" MALMERSTOKE
A famously indolent Society matron who is aunt to Cleone, and who has great insights to share about men, women and the world.

HENRY BANCROFT
A London exquisite whose arrival into their small town brings matters to a head between the unsophisticated Philip and the coquettish, dissatisfied Cleone.

SIR HAROLD BANCROFT
Henry's father, whose ill-timed visit led to Cleone's departure for London.

MOGGAT
Tom's dictatorial valet.

MRS. MOGGAT
Tom's housekeeper and ruler of his household.

FRANÇOIS
Philip's dictatorial, very excitable French valet. Despises Moggat.

JULES
Philip's groom, François' favourite victim.

MARIE-GUILLAUME
Philip's genius cook, cousin to François.

M. DE CHATEAU-BANVAU
An old friend of Sir Maurice's, he takes Philip in hand, and under his very accomplished wing, fitting him for Parisian society.

HENRI, COMTE DE SAINT DANTIN
A charming bon vivant who befriends Philip, becoming one of his closest friends in Paris, and does not take to Henry Bancroft at all, showing his good taste. Philip's second.

JULES DE BERGERET
Philip's other close friend, and his other second in his duel against Henry Bancroft.

PAUL DE VANGRISSE
Another friend of Philip's, bravely willing to listen to his poetry in order to watch his duel.

LE DUC DE VALLY-MARTIN
Another friend of Philip's.

CHARLES, VICOMTE DE RAVEL
A friend of Philip, fond of gossip and mischief.

CLOTHILDE DE CHAUCHERON
A lovely and vivacious Parisian beauty, much courted but not marriage material, says Philip.

JULIE DE MARCHERAND
Another of Philip's flirts; it was her pearl earring that fired him with creative fervour.

MADAME DE FOLI-MARTIN
Her jealous husband took exception to Philip's gallantry, leading to a duel in her honour.

HENRI DE CHATELIN
A good friend of Saint-Dantin, and big fan of Philip.

M. DE CHAMBERT
An acquaintance of Henry Bancroft, who acts as his second, but clearly prefers Philip.

LE VALLON
A friend of Henry Bancroft, who is his other second, with no love for Philip.

SIR DEREK BRENDERBY
An admirer of Cleone, to whom she briefly becomes engaged. A clever swordsman.

ANN NUTLEY
A London beauty to whom Philip plays mild court, to Cleone's fury.

SIR MATTHEW TRELAWNEY
Cleone compares him favourably with Philip.

LORD CHARLES FAIRFAX
One of Cleone's admirers, known to Philip.

~ | ~

"Don't interrupt my peroration, lad. They think you a noble—what was the word you used?—clodhopper. 'Tis marvellously apt."
— *Powder and Patch*, Chapter V

"I'll not listen to your verse on an empty stomach," declared the Vicomte. "Belike I shall appreciate it when in my cups."
— *Powder and Patch*, Chapter VIII

~ | ~

THE LOCATIONS

LITTLE FITTLEDEAN
Among the downs of Sussex, between Midhurst and Brighthelmstone
- **Jettan's Pride**
West of Little Fittledean, close to the London Road and Great Fittledean
- **Sharley House**
Within easy walking distance of the town centre.

LONDON
- Half Moon Street, home to Tom Jettan
- 14 Curzon Street, home to Philip Jettan

PARIS
- De Farraud's, where Philip confronts Henry Bancroft
- Hotel Cléone, the newlywed Jettans' Paris home

CELEBRITY SIGHTINGS

DOUGLAS, CATHERINE "KITTY," DUCHESS OF QUEENSBURY
(1701 – 1777) Wife to the 3rd Duke, she was Queen Anne's Lady of the Bedchamber, but was banned from Court by George II for being too "forward" in asking a favour. She was a patron of the arts known for her balls and masquerades, as well as her personal style and beauty. In her later years she was notable for retaining the fashion of her youth, as well as for, most unusually, often wearing an apron.

GEORGE IV OF ENGLAND
(1762 – 1830) Eldest of George III's children, the Prince of Wales grew up to be a young man of great wit and style, causing him to be nicknamed "the First Gentleman of Europe." An aesthete and gourmand, he became a byword for extravagance and decadence, as well as for his unhappy marriage to Caroline of Brunswick and poor political choices. Due to his father's ill-health, he was given the title of Prince Regent in 1811, which he maintained until his father's death in 1820, thus giving the Regency period its name. He was crowned George IV in 1821, and upon his death was succeeded by his brother, William IV.

JUVENAL
~ 1st & 2nd Century AD. Decimus Junius Juvenali was a Roman poet known principally for his collected work the *Satires*. He is something of an enigma, but highly regarded among scholars.

POISSON, JEANNE-ANTOINETTE, 1ST MARQUISE DE POMPADOUR
(1721-1764). Mistress of King Louis XV of France and awarded the title Marquise de Pompadour. She was appointed Lady in Waiting to Louis's queen, and was among his most trusted advisors right up until her death, though no longer his chief mistress.

~ | ~

No powder, no curls, unpolished nails, and an unpainted face—guiltless, too, of even the smallest patch—it was, thought Cleone, enough to make one weep. Nevertheless, she did not weep, because, for one thing, it would have made her eyes red, and another, it would be of very little use.
— *Powder and Patch*, Chapter II

"Oh, Philippe, thou art a rogue."
"So I have been told. Presumably because I am innocent of the slightest indiscretion. Curious. No one dubs you rogue who so fully merit the title. But I, whose reputation is spotless, am necessarily a wicked one and a deceiver. I shall write a sonnet on the subject."
— *Powder and Patch*, Chapter VII

~ | ~

WHAT A QUIZ!

Think you know your Heyer? These questions will test your knowledge...

1. Which publishing house first released *The Transformation of Philip Jettan*?
2. Who is the heroine of the novel?
3. Name Philip's faithful valet.
4. "Marriage for" what is the Jettan adage?
5. What is Cleone's flower, according to Philip?
6. What jewel is Philip's famous rondeau about?
7. Near which town is Jettan's Pride situated?
8. Who rules Tom Jettan's house?
9. What kind of musician is hired to attend Philip's duel with Bancroft?
10. To whom does Cleone become engaged at the Dering ball?

ANSWERS: 1. Mills & Boon; 2. Cleone Charteris; 3. Francois; 4. "love"; 5. a rose; 6. a pearl earring; 7. Little Fittledean; 8. his housekeeper, Mrs. Moggat; 9. a fiddler; 10. James Winton and Sir Deryk Brenderby

~ | ~

He discovered that it required the united energies of the three men to coax him into his coat. When at last it was on he assured them it would split across the shoulders if her so much as moved a finger.
"Forget it, little fool!"
"Forget it?" cried Philip." How can I forget it when it prevents my moving?"
— *Powder and Patch*, Chapter VI

WHAT THEY SAID

Contemporary Reviews of *Philip Jettan* and *Powder and Patch*

Sheffield Daily Telegraph, August 13, 1923

The Transformation of Philip Jettan by Miss Stella Marten [sic] is a very pleasing novel of the costume type, or rather of that school, which may be called "The Pimpernel." It is written simply but with some dramatic force, and while not pretending to any outstanding distinction, is a relief to the sex novels and those dealing with the mental and spiritual development of immature and uninteresting undergraduates, of which the public has of late been surfeited.

~|~

The Register, Adelaide, November 17, 1923

'A Comedy of Manners' is appended as a sub-title to the tale of handsome Philip's transformation, and comedy indeed it is. The comedy of a youth of the mid eighteenth century who transformed himself from a country bumpkin into a very polished man of the world—setting all Paris agog in the space of a brief six months, ogling and duelling and ruffling with the best of them, to the confusion of his lady and the amazement of his social sponsors and instructors. Philip is English by birth and French by pose and partial adoption, and with Monsieur Beaucaire of happy memory it was the other way about, but for all that there is often more than a hint of Beaucaire in Philip— once, indeed, a speech and situation that are almost literally Beaucaire. But Beaucaire was loveable enough to make welcome secure for his followers, and doubtless Mr. Tarkington will take the resemblance as that imitation (if imitation it be) which is the sincerest flattery.

~|~

Illustrated London News, July 28, 1923

The author described her story as "a comedy of manners" and indicated the period by the statement in Chapter I: Charles the Second was King." Whether the expression "way back' was used in the succeeding century may be doubted, but matters little. The hero is "transformed" from a country bumpkin to a fashionable blade of London and Paris who shines in Society and fights duels.

~|~

Aberdeen Press and Journal, June 22, 1923

A charming love story of the romantic type set in the days of duels and compliments. Philip, only son of Sir Maurice Jettan, refuses to follow the Jettan tradition and become a polished man of the world. He prefers to live in the country and act as squire on his father's estate. Philip loves Cleone, the daughter of a neighbour, but she is in league with Sir Maurice to make Philip a real gentleman, and tells him she cannot marry a country bumpkin. Philip accordingly goes to Paris and becomes the most dandified and frivolous member of the smart set, with a reputation for gallantry that eventually reaches Cleone's ears. In six months he returns to London, outwardly a powdered and painted doll. Much innocuous philandering and misunderstanding take place before the desired denouement is reached.

~|~

SELECTED COVER GALLERY

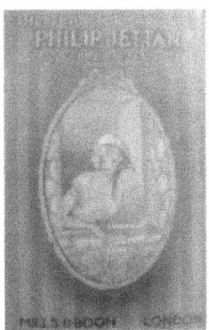
Mills & Boon, UK (1923)

Heinemann, UK (1930)

Pan, UK (1950)

Pan, UK (1952)

Pan, UK (1959)

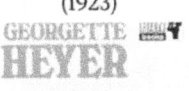

Pan, UK (1968)

Dutton, US (1968)

Bantam, US (1969)

Pan, UK (1976)

Bantam, US (1984)

Harlequin, Canada (2004)

Arrow, UK (2005)

Sourcebooks, US (2010)

Dover, US (2018)

Modern Library, US (2019)

SELECTED TRANSLATED EDITIONS

GERMAN: Zsolnay (1969)

GERMAN: Rowohlt (1986)

ITALIAN: Harlequin Montadori (2005)

POLISH: Harlequin (2007)

FRENCH: Milady (2015)

CLEONE: NAY OR YEA?

"NAY!" BY RACHEL HYLAND

ONE thing that is often remarked upon about Georgette Heyer's work is her seemingly innate ability to imbue her characters with verve and life, often in the space of only a very few words. In one or two sentences she can give us a fully realized publican, housekeeper or farmer's wife just as easily as she gives us a debutante, leader of fashion or peer of the realm.

The problem that goes along with that impressive skill, however, is that when the character she creates is just awful, that person springs off the page in all of their awfulness, and there is no escaping from it.

Such is the case with Cleone Charteris, the so-called heroine of *The Transformation of Philip Jettan*. Now, don't get me wrong, I am all for character growth, and character redemption. And our Philip is no pattern card of all the virtues either, it must be said. But honestly, every time I read this book, whether in Philip Jettan or Powder and Patch form (I alternate between the two, for some reason), all I can think about it how much I hate Cleone for the spoiled, inconsiderate, selfish little shrew that she is – so much so that I kind of think less of Philip for being so enamoured of her, when all she has to remotely recommend her is her apparently undeniable beauty.

I'm not sure I always hated her with such passion and vitriol. As a youngster reading this book – it was, and is, my mother's favourite Heyer, so it was one of the first that I read – I was more caught up in the splendour of the allegedly boorish Philip's Parisian makeover than I was in the woman who had caused it. Even now, those scenes of Philip's, ahem, transformation, are my favourite in the novel, as he learns all the shallow grace and insincere charm that were seemingly essential for any gentleman of the era. I do remember being delighted with his assorted flirtations, whether with women, poetry, or sword craft, and being saddened when his return to England was made necessary by the arrival of the hateful Henry Bancroft. (Another terrible person that comes to us fully realized at Heyer's already deft young hands.) Even then, I know I didn't think Cleone worthy of him, or of all his efforts to change himself for her benefit. But it is only in reading the book through adult eyes that you can see just how unsuited they are as a couple—not to mention how worthless she is as a person. Basically, to put it in Heyer terms, Cleone is *A Civil Contract*'s melodramatic, vain and entitled Julia Oversley, except that she unjustly gets her man.

Frankly, I'd have preferred Philip to end up with his own Jenny – the gentle and winning Jennifer Winton, another of his childhood friends – than the selfish, game-playing termagant simpleton who somehow won his untried heart, and with whom he will ever after be saddled. The fact that he fought duels for her! That he forsook everything he believed in for her! Why, Philip, why? Honestly, Cleone is the worst, and it is a testament to the outstanding nature of Heyer's enduring talent that, even despite this, I continue to voluntarily watch her get a wholly undeserved Happily Ever After.

Mostly, I think, because I do really love a good makeover.

"YEA!" BY JENNIFER KLOESTER

It is true that a surface reading of Cleone Charteris's character may see her judged as 'selfish, game-playing termagant simpleton' but even at the age of twenty, when she wrote *Philip Jettan*, Georgette Heyer knew to add depth and nuance to her heroine. A close reading reveals much about Cleone's life and upbringing that demands a greater degree of empathy than some readers have allowed.

An only child, Cleone enjoys a happy childhood romping, playing and quarrelling with the neighbours' children: Philip Jettan and James and Jennifer Winton, before she is sent away to a convent for 'a slight education': i.e. enough learning to fit her to become the wife of a well-bred man, to bear his children and run a household. On leaving the convent and before returning to her home in Little Fittledean – a small village, which must also be taken into account when thinking about Cleone's upbringing – she spends a few months with her aunt in London. There she is feted and petted and, along with the rest of the Beau Monde, learns to admire colour and style and to prefer 'her cavaliers to be à la mode'. Despite her success in Town and the adoring ways of Mr Bancroft on her return home, Cleone's head is never turned. It is Philip she loves with an unswerving loyalty and Philip she yearns for, but Heyer is clear in describing the conflict that keeps the two apart until both have changed and learned something of themselves and each other (note that both change, not only Philip):

> "She played with Mr Bancroft, but thought no less of Philip. Yet Philip continued to irritate her. His air of ownership, his angry, reproachful looks, fired the spirit of coquetry within her. Mastery thrilled her, but a mastery *that offered to take all, giving nothing*, annoyed her." [my italics]

Cleone is very much the product of her time and upbringing and if this comes across as selfish and demanding that's hardly surprising given that the social expectations of the era require her to submit to marriage before she had ever truly lived. Unlike Philip, who seems to hold nearly all the cards in this unequal relationship, Cleone cannot go off to London or Paris on a whim, or hang out with all sorts of people in gambling dens, or visit bordellos or even just turn up at the Royal Court. She can't learn to fence, go shopping alone, engage in a duel, or push the boundaries of propriety an inch! Her options are extremely limited. Cleone doesn't have the same freedoms as Philip because she is bound by expectation, rules and Duty far more than he will ever be. A limited education, her closeted life in Little Fittledean, being pampered and petted and raised to be a paragon of physical beauty and female virtue – her choices are few. Cleone's only power is to demand a husband who fits the social mores expected of a man (at least on the surface), just as she is expected to fit the pattern laid down for a female of birth.

She has so little power in her life. She loves Philip, but to simply give in to his demand that she love him exactly as he is, with no apparent thought of a life outside of the country village in which they live, of no fun, no fashion or balls or parties or intrigue – no romance! Cleone is right to demand something more. This is her only chance to wield the little bit of power she holds and who can blame her for doing so? She's already (secretly) determined to accept Philip and have him as her husband, but who can blame her for wanting him to be fabulous?

Obviously, Cleone can see Philip's potential. She wants him to comply with the social conventions – exactly as she is compelled to do. And why not? Why should it be one rule for Cleone and another for Philip, simply because he is a man? Were it not for Cleone, we should never have had Philip and his delightful makeover and Philip would never have expanded his horizons and become so much more than the untried, country-tied, ignorant man that he was.

Cleone is good for Philip. She loves him and wants him but she is not willing to sacrifice her own character to his demands. True, there are moments of selfishness and vanity, but one must also recognise the moments of humility, kindness and doubt. Cleone is very human and also very young. Her emotions are just what one might expect from a young woman torn between love and wanting social acceptance. In the end it is love that wins, for Cleone submits and even confesses her mistake in trying to change Philip, never mind that her demand forms the basis for the entire book and makes Philip a better man. He certainly sees her worth, for Philip loves Cleone above all other women; he sees her as she truly is and that, I think, tells us a lot about Cleone, too.

~ | ~

NONPAREIL

International Heyer Society Circular #4, October 2020

FROM THE PATRONESSES

Welcome once again to the monthly circular of the International Heyer Society!

It is our fourth edition, and here we celebrate Georgette Heyer's intriguing first contemporary novel, *Instead of the Thorn*. Don't miss Jennifer Kloester's insightful essay on this often-forgotten work, as well as our breakdown of the characters, literary references, locations, contemporary reviews and more. The trivia quiz is even more challenging than usual this time!

~|~

"My dear good child," he said, polishing his eyeglasses on a large silk handkerchief, "for heaven's sake cultivate some independence of thought! Don't repeat your aunt's views; let's hear your own. They're the only ones that are worth having from you."— *Instead of the Thorn*, Chapter 1

Stephen was silent; he did not want Cynthia to know how fascinated by Elizabeth he had been; he was fond of Cynthia, she was his pal, but she had a way of being sarcastic when you were not in the mood for sarcasm.
— *Instead of the Thorn*, Chapter 4

~|~

INSTEAD OF THE THORN

WHEN one thinks of Georgette Heyer, one does not ordinarily think of contemporary fiction, and one most certainly does not think of biting social commentary. Social satire to a degree, yes, and wisecracking humour, beyond a doubt. But *Instead of the Thorn* is so far outside the usual parameters of a Heyer novel that any reader coming to it late, especially any reader who adores her Georgian- and Regency-set romances, must surely question its authorship more than once throughout its pages.

My first time reading it made me more than a little uncomfortable, I will admit. There is just something so raw and revealing about it, from the abject fear of marital intimacy that it seems to reveal (entirely in the eye of the beholder) to the literary insecurity and snobbery that sees Heyer seemingly disdainful of her own earlier (and future) work.

Our ingenue heroine Elizabeth Arden is considered lacking in many ways, from her youth (hardly her fault) to her staid upbringing (hardly her fault), to her family (hardly her fault) to her lack of sex education (not entirely her fault), but it is evident throughout that her main flaw, in the eyes of both her fictional detractors and our author, is her allegedly poor taste in reading material. Elizabeth is not caught up on the "moderns," she enjoys romantic tales, and this is considered to be to her detriment. To me, this attitude goes a long way to explaining why *The Transformation of Philip Jettan* was brought out under a pseudonym, and is also the reason this book just makes me... sad. (Well, one of them, at any rate.) Nevertheless, it can only be considered essential reading for anyone seeking to understand Georgette Heyer, not only as an author (sorry, Stephen: writer) but also as the complex and fascinating person she most certainly must have been.

— *Rachel Hyland*

THE CHARACTERS

ELIZABETH ARDEN
Raised by her decorous aunt and rather indifferent father, she is swept off her feet by the debonair Stephen Ramsay at just nineteen, and has no idea what he – or the world – will expect from her as his wife. Confusion, conflict and compromise ensue.

ANNE ARDEN
Elizabeth's strait-laced aunt, who has cared for her since her mother's early death. Shocked by almost everything.

LAWRENCE ARDEN
Elizabeth's banker father leaves Elizabeth to Anne's care as he doesn't believe he knows anything about women. He is right.

MR. HENGIST
An old friend of Lawrence Arden's, he is the one person in Elizabeth's early life who clearly sees who she is. He's not always very nice to her, but his heart is in the right place.

SARAH COCKBURN
Neighbour and sort-of friend to Elizabeth, a modern girl who is impatient with the Ardens' old-fashioned ways.

MRS. COCKBURN
Her mother, a little confused by modern ways.

MARJORIE DREW
A school friend of Elizabeth's.

TONY DREW
Marjorie's brother, and Elizabeth's first crush.

MISS CARFEW
Smartly dressed and athletic.

MRS CARFEW
Her mother, hostess of Elizabeth's first dance.

CHUBBY
A most amusing youth, and Elizabeth's first dance partner.

CHARLES WENDELL
A bit simple, one of the idle rich; a war buddy of Stephen's who falls for Elizabeth and becomes her strongest supporter during her separation—because he wants her for himself.

STEPHEN RAMSAY
A sophisticate, writer and landowner of twenty-seven who falls for the nineteen-year-old innocent Elizabeth Arden and marries her, despite his family's objections. Confusion, conflict and compromise ensue.

CHARMIAN RAMSAY
Stephen Ramsay's charming and somewhat heedless mother, who is very kind to Elizabeth despite her doubts.

CYNTHIA RUTHVEN
Stephen's worldly sister, who is not at all kind to Elizabeth. Or anyone, really.

ANTHONY RUTHVEN
Cynthia's kindly husband, a gourmand.

CHRISTOPHER RUTHVEN
Their young son.

NANA
Stephen Ramsay's former nurse, now housekeeper. Thinks Stephen can do no wrong; very suspicious of Elizabeth.

NINA TRELAWNEY
Childhood friend of Stephen's and a fellow writer, Nina was clearly always intended for his bride. Has no love of Elizabeth.

JOHN CARYLL
Stephen's best man, pleasant but prone to quoting verses.

MRS. TRELAWNEY
Nina's mother.

MR. TRELAWNEY
Nina's father, a keen gardener.

LADY RIBBLEMERE
Leader of county society surrounding Queen's Halt, the Ramsays' home. Hates to disturb.

SIR GEORGE RIBBLEMERE
Her husband.

MRS. EDMUNSTON
Officious vicar's wife, serious about bridge.

MR. EDMUNSTON
The vicar, her husband.

MRS. FFOLIOT
A neighbour of the Ramsays'. Plays bridge.

MR. GABRIEL
Owns the farm in Wood End, where Elizabeth escapes for a month during troubles in her marriage. Full of wisdom.

MRS. GABRIEL
His wife. Has even more wisdom.

NELLIE
Their sheepdog.

EMILY
Their cow.

BERTIE TYRELL
A futuristic poet and noted eccentric, a close friend of both Stephen and Nina.

MRS. TYRELL
Bertie's equally eccentric, and artistic, wife.

LUCY ELMSLEY
Runs a private dance club, which Elizabeth joins through Sarah Cockburn.

MR. ELMSLEY
Her husband.

MRS. COTTON
Elizabeth's landlady at her London rooms.

FLO
Stephen's cocker spaniel.

HECTOR
Stephen's Irish wolfhound.

JERRY
Stephen's Airedale.

THOMAS
Mrs. Ramsay's much indulged bull terrier.

MR. HEMINGWAY
Worshipper of Nina Trelawney, becomes engaged to her. Does not appear in person.

~ | ~

"When you had a man with you these disturbances did not happen, or if they did you had nothing to do with them."   — *Instead of the Thorn*, Chapter 21

"I've come to the conclusion that reticence—is rather dangerous."
      — *Instead of the Thorn*, Chapter 28

~ | ~

THE LOCATIONS

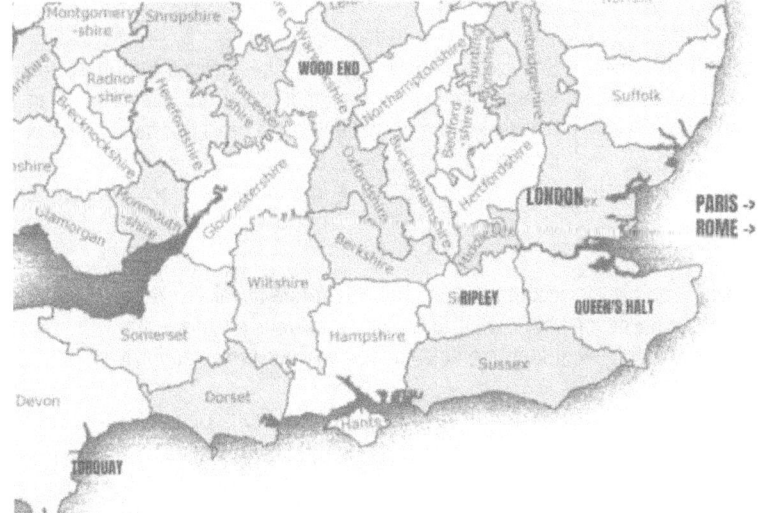

LONDON
- The Boltons, Kensington
- Hanover Square
- Victoria Station
- Knightsbridge Hotel
- Queen's Hotel
- Baker Street
- Bond Street
- Regent Street
- Hyde Park

QUEEN'S HALT
- The Ramsay estate, in Kent, "in a hollow beyond Cranbrook"

TORQUAY
On the coast of Devon.

WOOD END
- Gabriel's Farm

RIPLEY
A picturesque village in Surrey

PARIS

ROME

CELEBRITY SIGHTINGS

ALCOTT, LOUISA MAY
1832 – 1838. American novelist and poet most famous for the enduring novel Little Women and sequels. She also wrote lurid tales under the name A. M. Barnard. A noted feminist.

ARBITER, GAIUS PATRONIUS
c. 27 – 66. Roman courtier in Nero's time and believed to be the author of Satyricon, the second-oldest surviving Roman novel.

AROUET, FRANÇOIS-MARIE
1694 - 1778. Better known as Voltaire, this French Enlightenment poet, novelist, historian and philosopher is best remembered for his great, if brutal, satirical novel Candide.

BAKST, LÉON
1866 - 1924. Born Leyb-Khaim Izrailevich Rosenberg, he was a Russian artist and set designer most closely associated with the Art Nouveau and Modernist schools.

BEARDSLEY, AUBREY VINCENT
1872 - 1898. Artist and illustrator well known for his controversial and grotesque work in the style of Japanese woodcuts. He died of tuberculosis at the age of just 25.

BYRON, GEORGE GORDON, 6TH BARON
1788 - 1823. A Scottish peer and leading Romantic poet who first made his name with the epic poem Don Juan. His then-scandalous love life included multiple high-profile affairs (most famously with Lady Caroline Lamb, mentioned frequently in Heyer) and possible bisexuality. He died fighting in the Greek War of Independence, and is still a hero there. His daughter, Ada Lovelace, is considered the mother of modern computer science.

CHESTERTON, GILBERT KEITH
1974 - 1936. English writer, philosopher and critic best known for his Father Brown detective stories.

CONRAD, JOSEPH
1857 - 1924. A Polish-English modernist and author of often nautical-set novels chiefly remembered for the disturbing Lord Jim and even more disturbing Heart of Darkness.

DICKENS, CHARLES JOHN HUFFAM
1812 - 1870. English writer, publisher, editor and social critic. Despite his lack of formal education, Dickens is one of the most famous and revered of all English-language novelists. His fifteen novels include some of the most beloved in all literature.

DOSTOYEVSKY, FYODOR MIKHAILOVICH
1821 - 1881. Russian novelist most famous for his challenging works Crime and Punishment and The Brothers Karamazov.

GALSWORTHY, JOHN
1867 - 1933. English novelist and poet best known for his semi-autobiographical series The Forsyte Chronicles. Won the Nobel Prize for Literature in 1932.

HARDY, THOMAS
1840 - 1928. English realist novelist and poet fascinated by the countryside and/or tragedy, as evidenced by his pastoral novels Tess of the D'Urbervilles and Far from the Madding Crowd, et al. His poetry has not remained as well-known as his prose, but was greatly acclaimed at the time of its publication.

KIPLING, RUDYARD
1865 - 1936. Indian-born English writer known for his works set in Colonial-era India. He won the 1907 Nobel Prize for Literature, the first English-language and still youngest to do so. Notable works include Kim, Gunga Din and Mandalay, but he is perhaps best remembered as the author of The Jungle Book, on which the Disney animated film is based.

LESAGE, ALAIN-RENE
1668 - 1748. Enigmatic French novelist and playwright, known for his comedies.

MACAULAY, DAME EMILIE ROSE
1881 - 1958. Prolific novelist, biographer and travel writer whose work is often erroneously considered to be strongly moralistic in nature.

McKENZIE, SIR EDWARD MONTAGUE COMPTON
1883 - 1972. Compton McKenzie was a Scottish writer and politician best remembered for his comic novel Monarch of the Glen.

MEREDITH, GEORGE
1828 - 1909. English novelist and poet best remembered for his bleak work The Egoist.

MORRIS, WILLIAM
1834 - 1896. English textile designer, writer, illustrator, designer, activist and founder of the Arts and Crafts Movement.

SCOTT, SIR WALTER, 1ST BARONET
1771 - 1832. Famed Scottish historical novelist, playwright and historian best remembered for the sweeping epics Waverley, Rob Roy and Ivanhoe. By profession a lawyer and judge, he was made baronet in 1820.

SHAW, GEORGE BERNARD
1856 - 1950. Irish playwright who penned more than sixty plays, most notably Pygmalion (the basis for My Fair Lady) and Man and Superman. Shaw was also a radical, often misguided, thinker fond of eugenics. He was also an early anti-vaxxer.

SHELLEY, PERCY-BYSSHE
1792 - 1822. A leading and influential English poet of the Romantic school, he ran away with and married two different 16-year-old girls – one of them Mary Shelley, author of Frankenstein – and spent much of his short life in disgrace and near-penury.

SMITH, ELIZABETH THOMASINA MEADE
1844 - 1915. An Irish writer, as L. T. Meade she produced over 300 novels, many of them "girls' stories" aimed at young women, but her range was wide and included occult detective fiction, romance and historical works.

SMOLLETT, TOBIAS GEORGE
1721 - 1771. Scottish poet and author of picaresque novels.

SWINBURNE, ALGERNON CHARLES
1837 - 1909. English poet, playwright, novelist and critic known for his Classical imagery and subjects.

TENNYSON, ALFRED, 1ST BARON
1809 - 1892. English Poet Laureate for 42 years who was made baron in 1884. Still considered one of the world's great poets.

THACKERARY, WILLIAM MAKEPEACE
1811 - 1863. Indian-born English author and illustrator best remembered for Vanity Fair.

WARD, MARY AUGUSTA
1851 - 1920. Australian-born writer of so-called "improving" works, many for children, who published under the name Mrs. Humphrey Ward. Leading anti-suffragist.

WORDSWORTH, WILLIAM
1770 - 1850. English poet who was one of the founders of the Romantic school. Poet Laureate for seven years, he is notable for having penned no official verses. Often associated with the Lake District, where he was born and which he celebrated in many of his works, His lengthy work The Prelude was published posthumously to very little contemporary acclaim, but is now considered a masterpiece of autobiographical poetry.

YEATS, WILLIAM BUTLER
1865 - 1939. An Irish poet and, later, politician, his work is often considered a cornerstone of 20th century artistic expression. Awarded the Nobel Prize in Literature in 1923.

YONGE, CHARLOTTE MARY
1823 - 1901. English author of children's literature, widely considered to be of a moralistic tone founded in her ardent Christian faith. A strong advocate for public health, public works and proper sanitation.

~ | ~

"You know, he rules my life, which is sometimes tiresome. That's the worst of a dog—yes, and the best too—if you're really and truly fond of them you can't stir without them, and then where are you?"
— Instead of the Thorn, Chapter 9

She did not know Stephen. She realized that now, and thought that the love that survived seeing a man unwashed and unshaven before breakfast must be great indeed.
— Instead of the Thorn, Chapter 12

~ | ~

"There's so much I want to say, and I can't say it without sounding like a third-rate novel. I'd like to say all the things that I thought I should never say. I want to tell you that your eyes are like pansies, all velvety and soft, but I know quite well from the solemn look on your face that you'll think I'm just phrase-making."

— Instead of the Thorn, Chapter 9

WHAT A QUIZ!

Think you know your Heyer? These questions will test your knowledge...

1. In which year was *Instead of the Thorn* first published?
2. Name its heroine.
3. How many dogs does Stephen Ramsay have?
4. What is the name of the Ramsay family estate?
5. Who is Mr. Hengist?
6. At whose farm does our heroine take refuge from her marriage?
7. Name Stephen's childhood friend and fellow writer.
8. Where does our heroine first meet Stephen?
9. Who is our heroine's aunt?
10. Who is Mrs. Edmunston?

ANSWERS: 1. 1923; 2. Elizbeth Arden; 3; Queen's Halt; A friend of Elizabeth's father; Mr. and Mrs. Gabriels' farm; Nina Trelawney; At a dance; Anne Arden; The vicar's wife at Queen's Halt.

~ | ~

"When I see all these modern young minxes with their cigarettes and their backless gowns, I realize what a complete success Elizabeth's upbringing has been."
— *Instead of the Thorn*, Chapter 3

"She won't let Elizabeth have a mind of her own; she wants her to have her mind. Stephen, that's rather clever. Now I know where you get your brains from."
— *Instead of the Thorn*, Chapter 6

~ | ~

SELECTED COVER GALLERY

Note: No known international versions exist.

Hutchinson, UK (1923)   Small Maynard, US (1924)   Longman, UK (1929)   Longman, UK (1931)   Amereon House, US (2008)

~ | ~

"Rather outspoken, of course," he said. "Personally I like to hear a spade called a spade, though."
  "Undoubtedly," Cynthia replied, "but it is not always necessary to call it a 'bloody shovel.'"
— *Instead of the Thorn*, Chapter 17

"I should have thought you'd have run a mile sooner than meet her."
  "Oh, no, Cynny, not at my age and certainly not in this skirt."
— *Instead of the Thorn*, Chapter 23

WHAT THEY SAID

Contemporary Reviews of *Instead of the Thorn*

The Sketch, **December 12, 1923**

A story of these present dancing days. Elizabeth and Stephen danced and motored into sudden marriage. Elizabeth, although up to date in many ways, was a bit of a simpleton in essentials, and Stephen wasn't cut out for the role of Ideal Husband. Plenty of diversion, and a good deal of truth in this faithful picture of a certain set.

~|~

Sporting Times, **January 12, 1924**

It is pretty generally agreed in these days of advancement and progress that mothers should impart to their daughters at some time before marriage certain of the facts of life of which young women are popularly supposed to be ignorant. Miss Georgette Heyer apparently endeavours to support the agreement in her story *Instead of the Thorn*. The girl she portrays has not mother to instruct her, and the maiden aunt who adopts the maternal role adheres to the stupid convention of reticence. The result is that the girl Elizabeth goes to her bridegroom in a state of "innocence" – to use a much-abused word – and with no more knowledge of the ordeal she has to face than a child of ten possesses. The young husband proves to be a good sort, however, and though disaster comes early in their married life it proves to be temporary only and the broken course of true love is joined up again. Miss Heyer is somewhat stereotyped in plot and characterisation; but she can write. She needs to cultivate originality, and if she can do so will someday become a factor in popular fiction.

~|~

The Guardian, **November 29, 1929**

Instead of the Thorn tells of a stiff, sweet, lovely young "Puritan" girl who knows nothing of "life" and marries without realising what marriage means. She is hardly a new acquaintance, but it is less surprising to meet her when one realizes that she is being presented not in a new book but (as in this case) in the re-issue of an old one. Miss Georgette Heyer handles the pretty little lady very charmingly.

~|~

The Scotsman, **February 4, 1924**

Instead of the Thorn by Georgette Heyer is one of those now familiar studies of wedded life in which the girl marries a man whom she does not love, and without understanding what marriage really is, and both parties to the unequal contract reap the unfortunate consequences. Elizabeth has been trained up, so far as her nature allows, to be the "complete prude" under an early Victorian aunt. Years of bitterness, misunderstanding, and separation had to intervene before, largely through Stephen's Ramsay's patience and forbearance, almost unnatural in one of his ardent temperament, the real Elizabeth—"Elizabeth—pure and simple"—at length came through the Victorian shell; and all was peace and bliss in what had been a divided household. Mrs. Heyer sets out to prove a proposition, and of course, having all the materials in her hands, and having a skilful and discriminating touch, she proves it successfully.

HER FIRST CONTEMPORARY NOVEL BY JENNIFER KLOESTER

Georgette Heyer wrote her first contemporary novel in 1922, when she was nineteen. Her title for the book, *Instead of the Thorn*, is a reference to a line from the Biblical book of Isaiah: 'Instead of the thorn shall come up the fir tree, and instead of the brier shall come up the myrtle tree' and refers to the journey of self-discovery which the main protagonist, Elizabeth Arden, must undergo in order to grow and develop into her true self. Interestingly, the log-line beneath the cover picture of the first edition reads: 'A clever and intimate portrait of a modern married life, which should be read by every husband and wife who have failed to find happiness.' However, a marriage manual this is not! Certainly not to modern minds anyway. Maura Tan, writing about the contemporaries in the essay collection *Heyer Society* suggests that, 'if taken in a certain light, *Instead of the Thorn* reads kind of like a cry for help.' This is an understandable modern reaction to the novel and one which necessitates a brief summary of the characters and plot.

Elizabeth Arden has been raised by her repressed mid-Victorian aunt (a possible parallel to Heyer's own mother) and her tedious, narcissistic father. From childhood Elizabeth has been taught to repress her natural self, her curiosity and her intellect. Instead of growing up in an informed way, with an honesty of mind and self, she has learned to pretend – to become a 'humbug' as her wise would-be mentor, Mr Hengist, describes her early in the book. Throughout the novel he tries to help her, saying things like: 'You ask me what I really think. That would be the truth, Elizabeth—the thing you've run away from all your life.' Elizabeth grows up to be beautiful and, coming from the same affluent middle-class background as Heyer, does all the sorts of things Georgette would have done coming out in post-World War I London. She plays bridge, pays visits, entertains at home, goes to dances and meets people from the Bohemian set (with whom she is uncomfortable). Heyer once described herself as 'a sheltered daughter' and as someone who disliked 'Bohemians and studio parties', but there seem to be very few other similarities between Heyer and her naïve heroine. Indeed, although there are many moments in the book when one is tempted to think it is Heyer speaking for herself, these words are rarely uttered by Elizabeth Arden. At a dance Elizabeth meets famous author Stephen Ramsay who is entranced by her beauty and her virginal air, while she in her turn is enamoured of his good looks, sophistication and fame. In time, he proposes marriage and is accepted for all the wrong reasons. Stephen's anticipation of having Elizabeth as is wife is, to present-day readers – and very likely to the adult Heyer – nauseating.

> He thought of the treasures that were his to unfold, the frailty and the exquisite purity. Young and immature she was, too young and too sweet to hold alien opinions, young enough to be plastic, with intelligence to comprehend and absorb man's teaching. It would be joy to lay a guiding artist's hand on her mind still unformed, joy, greater still, to be sure, as he was sure, that no other man's lips had touched hers.

Heyer's novel is mainly about the ways in which Elizabeth subsumes her real self in order to conform to what she thinks other people and society expect of her, but it is also about an innocent young woman's experience of marriage and sex in a repressed age. As Jane Aiken Hodge has said, 'it was a bold book for an unmarried girl of twenty, especially in those inhibited days.' As the Dedication reveals, Heyer had spent many hours talking to her married friend, Joanna Cannan, about marriage, men and sex. In the novel, however, Elizabeth's maiden aunt in no way prepares her niece for conjugal love. Instead she sends her, like a lamb to the slaughter, to the altar and to the marriage bed, telling Elizabeth's father when he asks her to talk to his daughter about sex that:

> 'A great deal of nonsense is talked nowadays on this subject. Provided the man is nice it is most undesirable that girls should know too much. You may take it from me, Lawrence, that it simply puts silly ideas into their heads.'

Lawrence wanted to tell Anne that as she had never been married she knew nothing about it, but he dared not.

Consequently, Stephen and Elizabeth's relationship is sorely tested when she enters the marriage knowing nothing of sex only to find that she is utterly unprepared for its physical realities. Horrified and confused by the physical act and the emotional demands which marriage brings, at first she tries to meet her husband's and her family's expectations but gradually discovers that this requires an even greater self-deception. Eventually Elizabeth leaves the marriage and must face the world alone for a time while she learns to think and act as herself.

Contrary to her later opinion of *Instead of the Thorn*, the young Georgette was enthusiastic about her first contemporary novel, writing to her agent Leonard Moore from her hospital bed in 1923:

> Your letter is full of excellent news. I'm delighted to hear that the *Thorn* is coming out fairly soon. If Hutchinson is willing to put the book on Smith's stalls I think Daddy can do the rest. You see, he's closely in touch with the firm, and I think they'll do as he asks.

(Her father George had connections in both the literary and theatrical worlds and was Georgette's greatest supporter.)

Georgette also had strong ideas about the dustjacket:

> As to the wrapper, I'm really not strong enough to have another quarrel with Hutchinson about their artist's idiocy. I don't know what I want, but I think they'd better have Elizabeth on the jacket, and leave Stephen out of it. Elizabeth is like Emma Hamilton, only, of course, darker, and not so roguish. If they want to go in for symbolism they'd better have Aunt Anne and Stephen dragging the poor girl different ways. How awful! Failing that – I do have original ideas, don't I? – what about slicing Elizabeth in half, and making one half look Victorian, and the other modern? Don't slay me! I can't help it!

This idea is telling and reflects Georgette's recognition of the many seismic social and cultural shifts brought about by the Great War. An entire generation of young men had been killed, wounded or severely traumatised and a corresponding generation of young women had to navigate their way into and through a different kind of world. Many people were throwing off the restraints and shackles of the Victorian age and demanding a new kind of freedom. As a child of the Edwardian era, raised by Victorian parents, Georgette was also trying to work out what the post-War world meant for women like her. Elizabeth Arden is not Georgette Heyer, but it is through her that Heyer is attempting to shed light on many of the hypocrisies of the class system, intellectualism and the place of women in the new world. Through much trial and tribulation Elizabeth eventually attains a genuine understanding of herself and the effects of her stunted upbringing, and is able to claim a degree of personal freedom. She will never be entirely free, however, for Georgette knew that as a woman of her time, place and class there would always be shackles and restraints. It says much of Georgette Heyer's intellect and powers of observation that she could write so perceptively of marriage and a woman's lot at such a young age and while still unmarried herself.

– Jennifer Kloester

NONPAREIL

International Heyer Society Circular #5, November 2020

FROM THE PATRONESSES

Welcome once again to the monthly circular of the International Heyer Society!

Here we go in-depth into Georgette Heyer's first medieval novel, *Simon the Coldheart*, one of two historical outings she chose to withdraw from republication (for some reason). Don't miss Rachel Hyland's examination of our hero's many, many nicknames, as well as our breakdown of the characters, the historical personages, the locations, contemporary reviews and more.

> "My lord, it is my set purpose that I will take no honour, no power, no wealth, no title, that I have not earned by my own endeavour. I like not thine easy road, but all these things I will acquire, either by toil, by skill, or by valour." — *Simon the Coldheart*, Book I, Chapter IV

> "A murrain be on him! And when I came to him, what did I do? I did bow in all politeness, yet stiffly withal to show him I'd not brook his surliness."
> "I did hear ye did bow so low that your head came below your knees." — *Simon the Coldheart*, Book I, Chapter IX

SIMON THE COLDHEART

QUITE why Georgette Heyer felt the need to suppress this novel some decade or more after its first publication continues to be a mystery. With her four contemporary novels, and even her other historical novel so treated, it makes some sense. The contemporaries, published between 1923 and 1930, are very revealing, almost shocking in what they seem to say about their author, and by the time she suppressed them Heyer had become a famously private person. (An oxymoron?) Suppressing *The Great Roxhythe*, too, we can understand, as it is not a romance, not entirely successful as a history, and could be considered somewhat damaging to the brand she had by then established, as a writer of witty, clever, highly-readable fiction.

But *Simon the Coldheart*! Why suppress it, and not, for example, *Royal Escape* or *The Conqueror*, both of which were released in the 1930s and neither of which is nearly as captivating as this coming-of-age story of martial genius, determined stoicism, and a thawed cold heart? It might be argued that suppressing more recent novels would have been difficult, given that by the time *Royal Escape* was issued in 1938, Georgette Heyer novels routinely sold tens of thousands of copies upon release, but it's clear that would not have stopped her. Georgette Heyer was also, we know, always in need of money to pay her taxes and living expenses, so for her to have given up any source of revenue without strong cause is very puzzling.

Another reason the suppression of *Simon* continues to vex us is that it was George Heyer's favourite of her novels, which we know due to the dedication in the second edition, released after his death. From what we know of him, he was a well-read, discerning kind of man, so to dismiss his taste so thoroughly and decide to hide away a book he liked more than *The Black Moth* (for example) is perplexing. Whatever the reason, we can only be glad that her son, like her father, saw Simon's merits, and, alone of the six suppressed novels, overrode her judgment posthumously, calling his mother "her own sternest critic." Agreed!

— *Clara Shipman*

THE CHARACTERS

SIR SIMON OF BEAUVALLET, 1ST BARON
Illegitimate son of a noble, Simon enters the service of his father's sworn enemy at age fourteen. Quickly proving himself strong, valiant, quick-witted and good with weapons, he becomes a trusted squire, then soldier, then knight, then lord of the manor and advisor to the King. When sent to besiege her castle, he falls for the spirited Lady Margaret de Belrémy, who hates him. For a while, at least.

FULK, EARL OF MONTLICE
Nicknamed the "Lion," due to his tremendous lung capacity, he is won over by the young Simon's forthright manner and martial prowess, eventually coming to love him as a son. Possibly more than his own son, in fact.

SIR ALAN OF MONTLICE
Preferring gentler pursuits, Alan nevertheless finds himself a soldier alongside his one-time page, Simon. Nicknamed "Poet" by Henry V, he is a romantic and a dreamer, but also a brave officer and loyal friend.

SIR GEOFFREY OF MALVALLET
Simon's half-brother, the two meet as adversaries, but before long form a strong bond. A valiant knight, though reckless at times, he is one of Simon's trusted lieutenants.

GEOFFREY, EARL OF MALVALLET
Simon's father. Made no effort to find him, or provide for him until he is at Montlice. Grows as fond of him as he is of his legitimate son.

CHARLES, LORD OF GRANMERE
A London-based cousin of Fulk's, but far less intimidating, he is both well-liked and well-connected. Takes Simon under his wing.

ELEANOR, COUNTESS OF MONTLICE
Fulk's gentle wife.

ELAINE OF MONTLICE
Alan's sister.

JOAN OF MONTLICE
Alan's other sister, less comely than Elaine.

VINCENT
Captain of Montlice's men-at-arms; his death is a "blessing" according to Fulk.

GREGORY ARNOLD OF SAINT DORMANS
Simon's lieutenant at Montlice

ROGER OF MAITLAND
Simon's squire, prone to jealousy.

MALCOLM
Simon's other squire, object of said jealousy.

FRANCIS
Fulk's page.

MAURICE OF GOUNTRAY
Captain of Fair Pastures' men-at-arms, made Marshal of Beauvallet by Simon (even after an attempted stabbing of his boss).

CEDRIC OF GOUNTRAY
Maurice's impudent, adorable son, who begins as Simon's page and rises to be his squire.

HUBERT
Corrupt steward of Fair Pastures.

JAMES "SHORT LEG"
Hubert's sidekick.

HAROLD THE SMOOTH-TONGUED
Made Steward of Beauvallet after Hubert's banishment.

NICHOLAS
Captain of Fair Pastures' guards, a bully.

BASIL OF MORDAUNT
Made captain of Beauvallet's guards, following Nicholas' banishment

EDMUND OF FENTON
Elderly Marshal of Fair Pastures, forcibly retired by Simon.

WALTER OF SANTOY
Made captain of men-at-arms at Beauvallet, replacing Maurice.

BERNARD OF TALMAYNE
Secretary of Fair Pastures, and also Beauvallet.

ARNOLD
One of Simon's many pages.

EDMUND
Another page.

DONALD
Yet another page.

EDMUND MARNET
Simon's other squire.

JOHN TARBURY
Master of Works on the Belrémy campaign.

MASTER HUBERT
The surgeon of Simon's forces at Belrémy.

MALCOLM CLAYTON
A soldier of Beauvallet.

JOHN
A soldier of Beauvallet.

PETER
A soldier of Beauvallet.

FRANK
A soldier of Beauvallet.

JOHN OF BARMINSTER
Former baron of Fair Pastures, fought for Hotspur against Henry IV and was executed.

PAUL OF LENOIR
Lookout at Shrewsbury, envies Simon's eyes.

LADY MARGARET DE BÉLREMY
Comtesse, liege lady and leader of men (even into battle one time) she holds Belrémy in her own right, and is furious when her city falls to Simon. She is determined to be free of him, but she just can't seem to kill him, no matter how much she says she wants to...

JEAN, SIRE DE GALLEDEMAINE
Lady Margaret's trusted uncle and Marshal, father to the Chevalier de Fleuriel.

VICTOR, CHEVALIER DE FLEURIEL
Margaret's cousin, would like to marry her. Smarmy, snide and sneaky, he is not pleased when he discovers that Simon has an interest in Margaret beyond what his duty dictates.

JEANNE DE FAUCOURT
Sprightly, vivacious and quick-witted, she is Lady Margaret's closest friend and confidante, Persuaded to accompany Margaret on her flight from Belrémy, she longs for Geoffrey of Malvallet all the while, with whom she quickly fell in love. Likes to be mastered and does not believe in long engagements.

YVONNE DE VERTIMAINE
A "charmer" of Margaret's court who catches Alan's eye.

LÉON DE MARGRUTE
Lady Margaret's page. (Are all French pages called Léon?) Lady Margaret takes his pass to escape the castle; we can only hope he got to see his family another time.

HÉLÈNE DE COURVONNE
A lady-in-waiting to Lady Margaret.

AMÉLIE
Another lady-in-waiting.

ISABELLE
Yet another lady-in-waiting.

GASTON RANAUD
A kindly and formidable, red-bearded giant met by Lady Margaret and Jeanne on the road. He comes to their aid more than once, and later decides to take service with Simon. He really wanted to kill Raoul.

FERNAND DE TURINCEL
Lady Margaret's hope for salvation from the English hordes, but he has already submitted to Henry V in exchange for peace.

RAOUL THE TERRIBLE
His name pretty much sums him up. A depraved, despicable excuse for a human who threatens Lady Margaret and makes Simon lose his cool head for once.

~ | ~

CELEBRITY SIGHTINGS

DE BEAUCHAMP, RICHARD, 13TH EARL OF WARWICK
1382 – 1439. Soldier and statesman, knighted upon the coronation of Henry V, for whom he won significant victories in the Hundred Years' War. He oversaw Henry VI's education, and superintended the trial of Joan of Arc.

DE PERCY, HENRY, 1ST EARL OF NORTHUMBERLAND
1341 - 1408. Originally a supporter of Richard II, he switched sides to back Henry V, but then eventually rebelled against Henry on at least three separate occasions. He was convicted of treason, beheaded and his head put on a pike.

DE PERCY, SIR HENRY
1364 - 1403. Commonly known as "Hotspur" he was son of Henry de Percy and a valiant soldier who fought for Richard II, then Henry IV, then against Henry IV. He was killed at the Battle of Shrewsbury in 1403.

DE PERCY, THOMAS, 1ST EARL OF WORCESTER
1343 - 1403. Younger brother of Henry de Percy, he was made Earl by Richard II, whom he later helped depose in favour of Henry IV. Leader of the 1403 rebellion against Henry IV, he was beheaded for treason after its failure.

DE STAFFORD, EDMUND, 5TH EARL OF STAFFORD
1377 - 1403. A fourth son, he inherited the title at eighteen after his three elder brothers all died without issue. An adherent of Henry IV, he was killed at the Battle of Shrewsbury.

DE UMFRAVILLE, SIR ROBERT
1367 - 1437. A famed soldier who patrolled the Scottish border for most of his career, and carried out such successful raids of the north that he was nicknamed "Robin Mendmarket." He also accompanied Henry V to France and fought in the famed Battle of Agincourt. He died without children, the last of his name.

DOUGLAS, ARCHIBALD, EARL OF DOUGLAS
1391 - 1439. A Scottish peer and holder of many French titles as well, including a Duchy, he fought on the side of France during the Hundred Years' War and was a key official in the Scottish Court. He was made Regent for the child James II in 1437, which office he held until his death from fever just two years later.

GLYNDOURDY, GRIFFITH

1974 - 1936. Welsh: Gruffud Glyndŵr. Son of leading Welsh rebel Owain Glyndourdy (Glyndŵr/Glendower), he was captured in 1410 and died in the Tower of London, of the Bubonic Plague, two years later.

GLYNDOURDY, OWEN
1359 - c. 1415. Welsh: Owain ap Gruffud, Lord of Glyndyfrdwy, aka Owain Glyndŵr (usually anglicized to Owen Glendower) instigated the passionate, if unsuccessful, Welsh rebellion against English rule in 1400 and led his people for over a decade. Last seen in 1412, he is believed to have died in hiding in 1415. Became an almost mythical figure in Welsh folklore.

HENRY IV
1367 - 1413. Known in his youth as Henry Bolingbroke, at just 21 he joined in an attempt to check the perceived tyranny of Richard II, and was exiled. Upon the death of his father, a son of Edward III, in 1399, Richard II refused to turn over the duchy of Lancaster to Henry, so Henry rallied forces and took the throne. Though facing multiple rebellions at home, he still asserted his right to the throne of France, thus continuing the Hundred Years' War begun in 1337. His health failed in 1410 (he may have had leprosy), and his son took the reins of power.

HENRY V
1386 - 1422. Known as Henry of Monmouth, he made a name for himself on the battlefield while still a teen. Heading up the government following his father's illness, he continued to spend much of his life at war, either against rebellions at home or in the quest for the French throne begun by his great-grandfather, Edward III. After five years of famously brilliant campaigning, Charles VI of France agreed to a truce in 1420, marrying his daughter to Henry and designating him his heir, ending the Hundred Years' War. Two years later, Henry died suddenly and mysteriously just two months before Charles VI, so the French throne stayed in French hands, after all.

HOLLAND, JOHN, 1ST DUKE OF EXETER
1352 - 1400. Half-brother of Richard II, he was hot-tempered and murderous, but also fiercely loyal, after his fashion. Married to the future Henry IV's aunt, he was involved in the arrest of Henry's uncle, the Duke of Gloucester, and was punished by Henry IV with the loss of his recently acquired Dukedom (he went back to being Earl of Huntingdon). He was executed for his part in a 1400 rebellion against Henry.

HUNGERFORD, SIR WALTER
1378 - 1449. Soldier and statesman, he served as Speaker of the House of Commons, admiral of the fleet and Lord High Treasurer, among many other important appointments throughout his distinguished career. Supposedly once fought a duel with the King of France. He won.

LANCASTER, HUMPHREY OF, DUKE OF GLOUCESTER
1390 - 1447. "Son, brother and uncle of kings" he was Henry IV's youngest son. Scholarly and cunning, his opinionated manner led to frequent conflicts with powerful courtiers over the years, which gradually diminished his influence. His wife's 1441 trial for witchcraft saw him humbled, and he died just after a (probably false) accusation of treason.

LANCASTER, THOMAS OF, DUKE OF CLARENCE
1387 - 1421. Second son of Henry IV, he was left in charge of the English army in France where he died during an ill-planned battle against a combined French-Scottish force.

LUTTRELL, SIR HUGH
1364 - 1428. A consummate politician, he was advisor to John of Gaunt, Anne of Bohemia and Richard II, though his career flourished brightest under Henry IV and V. Ancestor of two American presidents, both Harrisons.

MONTAGU, THOMAS, EARL OF SALISBURY
1388 - 1428. A Henry V loyalist, he spent most of his adult life fighting in France. Killed by a cannonball during the Siege of Orléans.

MORGAN, PHILIP
? - 1435. A Welsh bishop, he journeyed with Henry V to France throughout his war there, and was appointed Chancellor of Normandy in 1418, following Henry's victory in the north of France. He was Henry V's personal chaplain, and also a diplomat.

RICHARD II
1367 - 1400. Succeeding to his grandfather Edward III's throne at the age of 10, he had a taste for peace and refinement, but his insistence on ignoring the advice of powerful lords led to a lot of trouble. It has been speculated that he may have suffered from a personality disorder, which led to a period of "tyranny," eventually resulting in his deposition at the hands of Henry V, whom he attempted to disinherit. He is believed to have starved to death while in prison.

SERLE, WILLIAM
? - 1404. An esquire to Richard II, he is believed to have stolen the dead king's seal to help maintain the illusion he was still alive. Betrayed by the calculating Henry de Percy, he was executed under extreme torture.

YORK, EDWARD OF, DUKE OF YORK
1373 - 1415. Grandson of Edward III, he died at the Battle of Agincourt. He is author of the oldest English-language book on hunting.

"I have never approached my goal through the back door, my lord, nor ever will. I march straight."
— *Simon the Coldheart*, Book I, Chapter I

"I observe thy folly," he said, "and know mine own wisdom. That is happiness."
— *Simon the Coldheart*, Book II, Chapter XXI

THE LOCATIONS

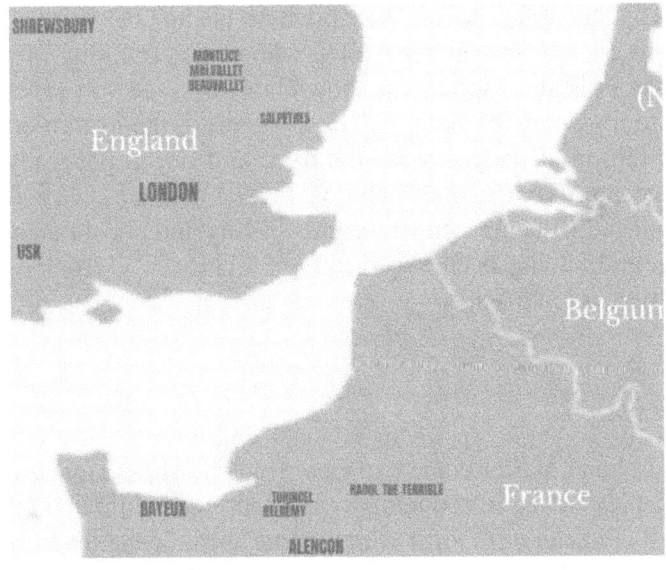

MONTLICE
Past Bedford and into Cambridge.
MALVALLET
Neighbour to Montlice.
BEAUVALLET
In Cambridge, to the south and east of Montlice.
SHREWSBURY
USK
On the border of Wales and England
SALPETRES
 - The Tavern of the Ox, into Suffolk from Cambridge
LONDON
 - The Lamb and Saracen's Head
 - Westminster Palace
 - Granmere Hall, the Strand
ALENCON
BELRÉMY
Between Argentan and Falaise, 25 leagues from Bayeux
TURINCEL
10 leagues from Belrémy
RAOUL THE TERRIBLE'S LANDS
To the south and east of Turincel
BAYEUX

WHAT THEY SAID

Contemporary Reviews of *Simon the Coldheart*

Times Literary Supplement, November 19, 1925

The historical novel has an appeal to two classes of readers: those who like a stirring tale of adventure, heightened by an infusion of "atmosphere," and those who are interested by a reconstruction of past times. Occasionally, but not very often, both are catered for by the same book. Of Miss Georgette Heyer's Simon the Coldheart one can only say it is above the average of the former class of romance, and that it does make an attempt, not completely successful, to enter the latter. The hero rather resembles one of those over-successful warriors portrayed by Henty, save that he is more gloomy and stern and less disinterested than most of them. He fights his way dourly upward from the moment when, a boy of fourteen, he forces his way into the service of the Earl of Montlice as a page, till he is finally appointed "Lieutenant and Warden of the Sands and Marches of Normandy" by Henry V. A little too dominating, perhaps, is Simon and the better, we should have thought, for being taught that the greatest sometimes must suffer defeat; but otherwise we have no fault to find with him. The heroine is rather less realistic, a shrew of shrews, who leads her men to battle, who attempts to stab her conqueror Simon in the back, who escapes from him in boy's clothes, and has to be rescued from the unspeakable Raoul the Terrible. Those who enjoy fighting at desperate odds, knowing that the best man will win, and in no doubt as to who is the best man, will be happy in Simon's company, though they may feel that the shrew and her tamer are an unconscionably long time in coming to terms. It takes us over 300 pages to reach the moment when the Lady Margaret stood by the sundial in her pleasaunce, gazing wistfully down at it. It was May now, and all about her flowers bloomed... The sun shone warmly down upon the garden, and the birds sung [sic], but the Lady Margaret was sad. Then we know all will be well, and that the sundial has not many minutes more of sadness to record.

~|~

The Sketch, October 14, 1925

By all the rules of the game in romantic fiction, the man nicknamed Coldheart must stand revealed, after due advance and regressions, as the ardent lover. Why pitch on the age of chivalry, if not to put a mettlesome knight through his paces? Simon Beauvallet, who comes trudging into the landscape to be made page to the son of Fulk the Lion, soon shows himself a lad of proper spirit. He begins by holding himself aloof from women, by being the happy warrior, the iron ruler, and so on. Then comes the moment when the proud lady crosses his path, and if you have any previous knowledge at all of the true romance, you will at once perceive that he and the lady will end by making a match of it. Simon lives in the fifteenth century, fights in England and France, wins promotion and honour from the King, and having been raised to high dignity as Warden of the Marches of Normandy, is left with his "tigress" in his arms.

~|~

Sydney Mail, February 24, 1926

A really good story of medieval England is to hand in *Simon the Coldheart* by that Miss Georgette Heyer whose *The Great Roxhythe* I had the pleasure of introducing to your notice a while ago on this page. Miss Heyer knows her period well, and can write of it with the true spirit of the lover of adventure. Here we have castles and keeps and villains and men-at-arms and all the rest of them.

And, of course, a beautiful and imperious young princess whose heart is won by the cave-man style so affected — and with such excellent results — by Miss Ethel M. Dell. And, lastly, *Simon the Coldheart* himself, the cave-man aforesaid, who has no time for women, but who turns the initial 'C' of his sobriquet to a 'G' in due course and marries the princess out of hand. A bold and stirring tale, my hearties!

~ | ~

SELECTED COVER GALLERY

Small Maynard, US
(1925)

Heinemann, UK
(1925)

Heinemann, UK
(1951)*

Heinemann, UK
(1978)

Pan, UK
(1979)

Fawcett, US
(1980)

Mandarin, US
(1992)

Amereon House, US
(1997)

Arrow, US
(1997)

Arrow, US
(2006)

Ulverscroft, UK
(2006)

Sourcebooks, US
(2008)

Wilder, UK
(2021)

German: Dtv
(1998)

~ | ~

SIMON THE [INSERT NICKNAME HERE] BY RACHEL HYLAND

"If my lord hath called thee names, then doth he love thee indeed." – Simon, about Fulk

Throughout the works of Georgette Heyer she proves herself a big fan of bestowing nicknames upon her characters. From the Nonesuch to the Incomparable, from Noddy to Satanas, from Kitten to Sparrow, rare is the Heyer book without some evocative sobriquet given to one or more of our new friends and acquaintances, universally acknowledged or privately held.

Of course, this is hardly unusual among, well, people. The practice has doubtless been around as long as there have been names, as long as there has been language. Indeed, when you think about it, names probably started as nicknames, and then just stuck, the way surnames in the Anglo-Saxon tradition often come from people's old timey jobs. (There were a lot of millers, carters, coopers and, apparently, smiths back in the day.)

And we only have to look at some of the real-life nicknames just from the Regency era - Silence, the Arbiter, Golden Ball, the Sprite - to see that this commonplace practice was most assuredly in regular use even among the exalted circles in which Heyer mostly lays her scenes. Some are endearments, some criticisms, some expressions of respect, some (perhaps most) are outright mockery. But all appeal to the very human desire to label others, for good or for ill, but even more, the desire to be part of the collective consciousness. The be in the know. To be in on the joke.

In *Simon the Coldheart*, Georgette Heyer takes this tendency of hers, and of ours, to the very, utmost extreme. Before the first chapter is out Simon has been called:

- springald
- cockerel
- my young spring-chicken
- babe
- bantam

and, oddest of all:

- my little fish

several of these occurring even after he has introduced himself by name to the man from whom he has come to seek employment. Imagine going to a job interview and being called someone's little fish! And it does not stop there, not by a long shot. (Not even a shot as long as our superhuman Simon can make with an arrow loosed from his trusty bow.)

That trove of aliases is Fulk, Earl of Montlice, better known (of course) as Fulk the Lion, a huge hulk of a man, his roar legendary, his temper ever uncertain. That he is fond of Simon is made amply apparent by his continued use of many and varied pet names throughout, from "young cockalorum" and "cold-blooded tiger-cub" to "self-willed puppy" and "Master Stiff-Neck," and a lot more besides.

But his sweetest nickname is probably the simplest. "My Simon." Fulk really loves his Simon like a son, and it is through these means that Heyer shows us the depths of his affection.

Fulk is not the only one giving Simon descriptive appellations, however. Henry of Monmouth, the future Henry V, explains it best, just after their victory over the Welsh rebels at Usk, in 1406. Simon had defeated the son of the rebellion's leader, one Gruffud Glyndŵr (known in Simon as Griffith Glyndourdy), in single combat, and Henry asked what he wanted in return. Simon could have asked for his ransom, or for land, or for, like, a pony. Instead, he asks for young Glyndourdy's armour, which is fancy and golden and very well made.

> "Thou shalt have it then," Henry promised. "Simon of the Gilded Armour!" He laughed, linking his arm in Simon's. "Verily, I do believe it is a new title thou seekest! Already I have heard tell of Simon the Lynx-Eyed, Simon the Coldheart, Simon the Lion, Simon the Soft-Footed, and I know not what beside. Whence come these names, Simon?
> "From foolish men's tongues, my lord," Simon answered.
> "Then shall I be foolish," Henry said, "for I shall call thee Simon the Silent."

That is not the only nickname Henry will bestow upon Simon. He is clearly as prone to the practice as Fulk, and even gets Simon's friends Geoffrey of Malvallet and Alan of Montlice in on the action:

> "What a trio I have about me!" he said. "My Soldier, my Knight and my Poet."

We then learn that the Duke of Clarence once dubbed the three "Iron, Flame and Silver." Really, was ever a Heyer novel more replete with this pleasing, even heart-warming, convention? The only mystery is how, from all of Simon's many monikers, it was "Coldheart" that our author selected for his titular one.

But, wait, is it a mystery? For all that the romance is very slow to come about, and we don't even meet our heroine until halfway through the novel, there are foreshadowing near-prophecies of the imminent melting of that cold heart at many times throughout the earlier chapters. How different might the book have seemed, though, had she used yet other nicknames, like *Simon the Iron Lord* or *Simon the Just*? We shall never know. Nor need we.

Simon the Coldheart suits it best.

— *Rachel Hyland*

~ | ~

WHAT A QUIZ!

Think you know your Heyer? These questions will test your knowledge...

1. In which year was *Simon the Coldheart* first published?
2. How old is Simon when the story commences?
3. Who is married to Fulk?
4. Who does Simon save at the Battle of Shrewsbury, which leads to his knighthood?
5. What is the original name of the estate Simon is gifted by Henry IV?
6. What is a nickname that Henry V bestows on Simon?
7. Who begins as Simon's page, and then becomes his squire?
8. Who tries to stab Simon in the back (literally)?
9. With whom does Sir Geoffrey of Malvallet fall in love?
10. Who said the above quote?

ANSWERS: 1. 1925; 2. 14; 3; Eleanor, Countess of Montlice; his half-brother, Sir Geoffrey Malvallet; Fair Pastures; "Simon of the Gilded Armour," "Simon the Silent," "My Soldier,"; Cedric of Gountray; Lady Margaret de Belrémy; Jeanne de Faucourt; Sir Alan of Montlice.

NONPAREIL

International Heyer Society Circular #6, December 2020

FROM THE PATRONESSES

Welcome once again to the monthly circular of the International Heyer Society!

Here we go in-depth into *These Old Shades*, a novel intended as a sequel to *The Black Moth*, except that it is not a sequel at all, more a reimagining, or reboot. Don't miss Jennifer Kloester's fascinating account of the book's journey to publication, or the comprehensive listing of the many historical personages that populate the novel. And, as always, there are reviews, locations, character bios and more.

~ | ~

"I trust you are satisfied with the King's appearance?"
"Oh yes, he is just like the coins!"
— *These Old Shades*, Chapter V

"There are many sins, *ma belle*, but only one that is unforgivable. That is vulgarity."
— *These Old Shades*, Chapter XIIII

~ | ~

THESE OLD SHADES

When I give talks on Georgette Heyer and people come up to chat with me afterwards, I find the book that is mentioned most often is *These Old Shades*. It regularly appears in the lists of 'Favourite Heyer Novels'. It was first published in 1926, was immediately popular, and it has never been out of print.

I have to admit that my first reading in my teens was not a great success. The Duke of Avon seemed so old and there was just too big an age gap between him and Léonie for my teenage mind to cope with. I think I read it once and never went back to it.

Then in my 30s I fell in love with the story. I loved the settings in Paris and other French towns, I really enjoyed the revenge aspect of the plot, and who could fail to fall in love with feisty Léonie? Most of my Heyer reading had been the Regency novels, and I found it very easy to envisage sexy heroes in the tight breeches, Hessian boots and superbly tied neckcloths of that era. The Duke of Avon's attire, however, took a bit more getting used to – high heels, jewellery, powder and wigs just didn't, at first, seem very masculine. But as the Duke is such a wonderful character, he too won me over, in spite of his outfits.

My journey to loving *These Old Shades* was a rather slow one. However, unlike many Heyer readers, I would still not place this novel in my Top Ten List. I prefer *Devil's Cub* about Dominic, Marquis of Vidal, who is the son of Léonie and her Duke, and I find that it's not a novel I go back to as often as I revisit others. I can't explain this preference, and I'm sure many members of the International Heyer Society will disagree with me, but, as Léonie would say: "Bah, *chacun a son goût!*".

— *Susannah Fullerton*

~ | ~

THE CHARACTERS

JUSTIN ALASTAIR, DUKE OF AVON
Dissolute, cynical and suave, he is renowned for his seeming omniscience and his killer wit. Out for revenge on the man who dared humiliate him decades earlier, he is drawn to the waif-like Léon, who reminds him strangely of someone…

HUGH DAVENANT
Avon's best friend and voice of reason, he is a kind and righteous man who is often outraged. Very fond of Léon, and later, Léonie.

LADY FANNY MARLING
Beautiful, vain and somewhat shallow, the winsome Lady Fanny is devoted to fashion, her husband, her brother and Léonie, in that order. She is a stellar hostess.

EDWARD MARLING
Lady Fanny's staid husband who has a soft spot for Léonie, despite himself.

JOHN MARLING
Their son.

LORD RUPERT ALASTAIR
Avon's scapegrace, ever-amusing younger brother, he becomes Léonie's first real friend.

ANTHONY, LORD MERIVALE
A neighbour of the Alastairs, he and the Duke had a falling out when Avon abducted the woman he loved. Léonie heals the rift.

JENNIFER, LADY MERIVALE
Once the object of Avon's – and many other gentlemen's – affection, she is now very content with her family life in the countryside.

JOHN MERIVALE
Their young son.

GEOFFREY MOLYNEUX MERIVALE
Their infant son.

MADAM HARRIET FIELD
A poor relation of the Alastairs', pressed into service as Léonie's chaperone at Avon Court.

RACHEL
Lady Fanny's lady's maid, fond of colourful expressions.

POMPEY
Lady Fanny's page.

JOHNSON
Butler at Avon Court.

COGGIN
Blacksmith at the village of Avon.

FLETCHER
Landlord of the Avon Arms.

MR. MANVERS
Missing a horse, thanks to Rupert. Furious.

GASTON
Avon's fussy, corpulent valet.

MEEKIN
Avon's groom.

LÉON/LÉONIE
Just nineteen, Léonie has been forced to dress as a boy for seven years. Pressed into service as the Duke of Avon's page, she later becomes his ward and is introduced to Paris society. Avon hopes she will make a suitable match, but other men do not interest her…

JEAN BONNARD
Léonie's hateful, jealous brother who forces her to dress as a boy and sells her to Avon. Again, he sells his sister. Keeps an inn in Paris.

CHARLOTTE BONNARD
His equally awful wife.

CURÉ DE BEAUPRÉ
The kindly spiritual leader of the village where Léonie grew up, he was tasked to teach his literacy, unusual in a peasant girl. Scion of an aristocratic house, committed to his faith.

HENRI, COMTE DE SAINT-VIRE
Disappointed of an heir, he swapped his daughter for a farm labourer's son in order to keep his despised brother from inheriting his estates. Fond of abduction, and other crime.

MARIE, COMTESSE DE SAINT-VIRE
His haunted, sickly, brow-beaten wife.

HENRI, VICOMTE DE VALMÉ
A "half-witted bumpkin," according to his uncle, he does not like to be at court and would prefer to be in the country, farming. Because a love of animal husbandry is hereditary, apparently.

ARMAND DE SAINT-VIRE
The Comte's friendly, popular younger brother, who dislikes his "nephew" and wants the title for himself. Fond of Avon.

DUCHESSE DE BELCOUR
Saint-Vire's sister, with whom Avon was infatuated as a youth., and the indirect cause of the animosity that exists between them.

DE FAUGENAC
A satellite of Saint-Vire's who makes a bid for Léon. Would die for his wife, he claims.

JEAN
The landlord of the Black Bull at Le Dennier, where Rupert and Léonie seek refuge.

MARTHE
His tender-hearted wife.

WALKER
The strict, very dignified butler at Avon's home in Paris. Looks like a camel.

MADAME DUBOIS
Fat housekeeper of Avon's French home, with a love of Leon.

GREGORY
A footman at Avon's home in Paris.

JACQUES
Another footman.

FREDERICK, LORD COLEHATCH
Hugh's deplorable brother, once loved Fanny.

CHEVALIER D'ANVAU
A friend of Hugh Davenant's.

VICOMTE FLORIMOND DE CHANTOURELLE
A friend of Avon's. Fond of bright colours and gossip.

DE CHÂTELAT
A friend of Merivale's and his host in Paris.

LOUIS CHATEAU-MORNAY
Plays dice with Avon at Vassaud's; Léonie brings them wine.

CORNALLE
Plays dice with Avon at Vassaud's.

RAOUL DE FONTANGES
A friend of Lady Fanny's.

DUCHESSE DE LA ROQUE
A fixture in French society.

M. DE LA VALAYE
An admirer of Léonie's.

MADAME DE CACHERON
Holder of parties.

MADAME DE MARGUÉRY
Player of cards.

D'AIGUILLON
Avon's friend.

MARRIGNARD
Among the fortunate who danced with Léonie.

LAVOULÈRE
A foppish gentleman impressed with Avon.

CHEVALIER DE SALMY
He mislikes Avon's strange eyes.

MARQUIS DE CHOURVANNE
Thinks Avon is a poseur.

MARQUISE DE CHOURVANNE
Probably likes Avon more than her husband.

MARCHERAND
Plays piquet with Saint-Vire and Hugh.

CLOTHILDE DE VAUVALLON
A dear friend of Fanny's.

MADAME HENRIETTE DE VERCHEREUX
Avon's spurned mistress who causes trouble.

MADAME DE DEFFAND
A very amusing lady; holder of explosive poetry readings.

M. DE LA DOUAYE
Poet, dazzled by a flower in Léonie's hair.

M. DE FOQUEMALLE
Writer of fulsome romantic periods.

MADEMOISELLE DE CLOUÉ
Lady in puce.

MADEMOISELLE BEAUCOUR
Intrigued to hear a fairy story from Avon.

MARIE
Léonie's maid.

CELEBRITY SIGHTINGS

BENTINCK, LORD GEORGE
1715 - 1759. Second son of the 1st Duke of Portland, he rose to the rank of major-general in the army before being elected as an MP in 1742, where he served until his death. Great-great-great-great-granduncle of Elizabeth II.

CAVENDISH, WILLIAM, 3RD DUKE OF DEVONSHIRE
1698 - 1755. Ascended to the title in 1729. Statesman, soldier and one-time Lord Lieutenant of Ireland. Father of seven children and common ancestor of Charles, Prince of Wales and Lady Diana Spencer.

CHARLES "III" OF ENGLAND
1720 – 1788. Charles Edward Louis John Casimir Sylvester Severino Maria Stuart was the great-grandson of James II and claimant to the throne of England. Also known as "the Young Pretender" and "Bonnie Prince Charlie," his various rebellions all failed and he died in exile.

CHEVIGNARD, ANNE-THÉODORE, COMTE DE TOULONGEON
1687 - 1771. Skilled diplomat and French ambassador to London, Lisbon, Copenhagen and various other European courts.

CIBBER, COLLEY
1671 - 1757. Actor, playwright and Poet Laureate. Remembered chiefly for not being considered a very good writer.

COVENTRY, GEORGE, 6TH EARL OF COVENTRY
1722 - 1809. Ascended to the title in 1752, the same year he married famous beauty Maria Gunning.

CROMWELL, OLIVER
1599 - 1658. General, statesman, and chief architect of the brief republican period in English history, after he deposed Charles I and was declared Lord Protector. A strict Puritan, laws under Cromwell were oppressive, and repressive, and genocidal towards Catholics. He died of malaria and was buried in great state, but after the restoration of the monarchy under Charles II he was exhumed and posthumously executed, hung as a traitor.

DE BOURBON, LOUIS-AUGUSTE, DUC DU MAINE

1670 - 1736. Favourite son of Louis XIV, by his "official" mistress, Madame de Montespan, he and his six royal siblings were legitimized, and he was showered with grand titles and wealth. Following Louis's death, he joined a conspiracy against the Duc d'Orleans, and was imprisoned.
DE BOURBON, LOUIS CHARLES, COMTE D'EU
1701 - 1775. Grandson of Louis XIV, he was a landholder and philanthropist who had little taste for court life. Remained unmarried and childless (as did his siblings) all his life.
DE BOURBON, LOUIS JEAN MARIE, DUC DE PENTHIÈVRE
1725 - 1793. Grandson of Louis XIV, he was a close friend of Louis XV. At the age of 12 he inherited his father's dignities, which made him Admiral of France, Governor of Brittany, Grand Huntsman of France, and much more. He was one of the richest men in Europe, a known philanthropist, and was the father-in-law of Philippe Égalité, the Duc d'Orléans, who supported the French Revolution but was beheaded anyway. An avid watch collector.
DE BOURBON, LOUIS JOSEPH, PRINCE OF CONDÉ
1736 - 1818. Succeeding to his title at the age of 4, the prince would become a general in the army as well as taking on the prestigious role of grand maître in the royal household. After his first wife's death he fell in love with Maria Caterina, Princess of Monaco, and the two lived together illicitly, much to her husband's displeasure. Following the Revolution he commanded an army of émigrés determined to take back France. The Condé Army disbanded in 1801, after 10 fruitless years. 14 years later, with Napoleon defeated, he returned to Paris.
DE LORRAINE, CHARLES, COUNT D'ARMAGNAC
1684 - 1751. Hereditary Grand Squire of France, he was count of both D'Armagnac and Brionne and known as Monsieur le Grand.
DE LORRAINE, LOUIS, PRINCE OF BRIONNE
1725 - 1761. Soldier, governor and also Grand Squire of France, after his cousin Charles above.
DE NOAILLES, MARIE VICTOIRE SOPHIE, COUNTESS OF TOULOUSE
1688 - 1766. The thirteenth of twenty children, she married an illegitimate son of Louis XIV and became a countess, but also five duchesses as well. Ancestor to the modern Brazilian, Belgian and Bulgarian royal families.
DE VIGNEROT DU PLESSIS, ARMAND, DUC DE RICHELIEU
1696 - 1788. Soldier, diplomat and notorious womanizer, to the extent that two ladies even fought a famous duel over him in 1721. Great-great nephew of Cardinal Richelieu, of The Three Musketeers fame.
DOUGLAS, WILLIAM, 4TH DUKE OF QUEENSBURY, AKA LORD MARCH
1724 - 1810. Cousin to the 3rd Duke, he was also Earl of March and Ruglen. Later fondly known as "Old Q", he was famous for his love of gaming. He never married but had a daughter, Maria, who wed the Marquess of Hertford in 1798. and was the Duke's principal heir.

FOUQUET, CHARLES LOUIS AUGUSTE, DUC DE BELLE-ISLE
1684 - 1761. Redeemed his disgraced family through martial prowess and diplomacy skills. Ruler of the city of Metz, which he greatly improved through public works.
FOUQUET, NICOLAS, MARQUIS DE BELLE-ISLE
1615 - 1680. Statesman and one-time favourite of Louis XIV, he died in prison after being accused of lèse-majesté, among other crimes.
GARRICK, DAVID
1717 - 1779. Actor, playwright and producer, pupil of Dr. Johnson, his natural style influenced English theatre for generations.
GUNNING, ELIZABETH
1733 - 1790. An Irish beauty of no fortune who wed the Duke of Hamilton and the Duke of Argyll. Created a Baroness in her own right.
GUNNING, MARIA
1732 - 1760. Sister to Elizabeth, the beautiful Maria wed the Earl of Coventry in 1752.
HAMILTON, JAMES, 6TH DUKE OF HAMILTON
1724 - 1758. Succeeded to the title in 1743. The first husband of Elizabeth Gunning, he died at the age of 33 from a cold.
JAMES "III" OF ENGLAND
Nicknamed The Old Pretender, he was the legitimate Stuart heir to the throne and styled himself King, though he was never crowned. He and his followers, believing in his divine right to rule, attempted to oust the Protestant William and Mary, with the support of Louis XIV and the Pope, though this was eventually withdrawn. Father to Bonnie Prince Charlie.
JOHNSON, DR. SAMUEL
1709 - 1784. Poet, playwright, essayist, critic and much else, he is best remembered for his mighty work, A Dictionary of the English Language, which was the definitive work on the subject for more than 150 years. Popularly believed to have penned it alone, he actually employed several assistants for the many years it took to complete.
LESZCZYŃSKA, MARIA KAROLINA ZOFIA FELICJA, QUEEN OF FRANCE
1703 - 1768. A Polish princess married to Louis XV when she was 22 and he 15. She was Queen of France for 42 years, longer than any other in that country. A devout Roman Catholic, she was beloved of the French people and was known for her generosity and patronage of the arts. Mother of ten, grandmother of three kings: Louis XVI, Louis XVIII and Charles X.
LOUIS XV OF FRANCE
1710 - 1774. Known as Louis the Beloved, be succeeded to the throne at the age of 5. His reign was marred by corruption and many wars, but was also distinguished by elegance. Keeper of too many mistresses to count, father of two dozen children, grandfather of 3 kings.
LOUIS, DAUPHIN OF FRANCE
1729 - 1765. Studious and devout, even though he was heir to the throne he was kept out of political affairs by his father, Louis XV. Married twice, he fathered 3 kings while never ascending to the throne himself, dying of tuberculosis at age 36.
NASH, RICHARD "BEAU"

1674 - 1761. Though both a solider and a barrister, he is best remembered as a leader of fashion, especially in the spa town of Bath, where he served as Master of Ceremonies for almost 60 years; he served the same post in Tunbridge Wells for nearly 30 years. Both were unofficial. He was a gambler always in debt, and inspired such devotion in his mistresses that one of them even lived in a hollowed-out tree for many years, distraught over their break-up.
PELHAM-HOLLES, THOMAS, 1ST DUKE OF NEWCASTLE
1693 - 1768. Statesman, two-time Prime Minister and frequent power behind the throne, he is best remembered for being kind of a jerk.
POISSON, JEANNE-ANTOINETTE, 1ST MARQUISE DE POMPADOUR
1721-1764. Mistress of King Louis XV of France and awarded the title Marquise de Pompadour. She was appointed Lady in Waiting to Louis's queen, and was among his most trusted advisors right up until her death.
PULTENEY, WILLIAM, 1ST EARL OF BATH
1684 - 1764. Politician. Served in the House of Commons for 35 years until made an Earl by George III, after which he relocated to the House of Lords, where he served until his death.
REYNOLDS, SIR JOSHUA
1723 - 1792. The leading portraitist of his day, he was a founder of the Royal Academy of Arts and official painter to the King. He lost vision in one eye in his later life and was forced into retirement at the height of his career.
SELWYN, GEORGE AUGUSTUS
1719 - 1791. Wit, politician, and great friend of Horace Walpole, with whom he shared a frequent correspondence. Despite his reputed intellect, he spent 44 years in the House of Commons without making a speech. An avid member of the Hellfire Club, he had a keen interest in the macabre and loved executions.
SHERIDAN, RICHARD BRINSLEY BUTLER*
1751 - 1816. Irish satirist, playwright, poet and theatrical producer, he owned the Theatre Royal, Drury Lane and is best remembered for his plays The Rivals and The School for Scandal. Less famously, he also sat in Parliament for 32 years. He died in poverty after refusing £20,000 from the American Congress, which he had supported.
STANHOPE, PHILIP, 4TH EARL OF CHESTERFIELD
1694 - 1773. Statesman and diplomat famed for his wit and dark eyebrows. A brilliant speaker and strategist, he was able to bridge divides and bring about social change, while at the same time at loggerheads with George II, from whom he declined a dukedom. He is best remembered for the letters full of worldly advice he sent to his son and godson. across several decades.
STEPHEN OF ENGLAND
c. 1092 - 1154. Fourth Norman King of England, his reign was beset by rebellions and civil wars. He was at last forced to declare his cousin Henry his heir over his own younger son to save the peace, following the sudden death of his eldest, Eustace, for whom he had been staunch in his defence of his crown.   King   Eustace.   Hmm.

* Here Heyer made one of her rare errors with this historical reference. It is doubtful that Sheridan was writing plays at the age of 4 or 5. (*These Old Shades* occurs in 1755-56, as other events and references establish.)

~ | ~

"Your conversation is always so edifying, Rupert. Yet I believe we can dispense with it."
— *These Old Shades*, Chapter XXIII

"If it were not Avon one would go away, but since it is he one stays."
— *These Old Shades*, Chapter XXXI

THE LOCATIONS

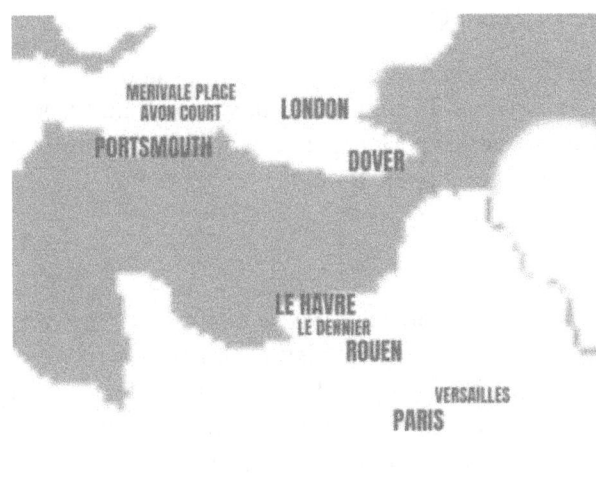

PARIS
- Hôtel Avon, Rue St. Honore
- The Crossbow, Rue de Sainte-Marie
- Vassaud's, a gaming house
- Maison Chourval, a house of ill-repute

VERSAILLES

LE HAVRE

LE DENNIER
Between Le Havre and Rouen.

ROUEN

BASSINCOURT
In Anjou, six or seven miles to the west of Saumur

LONDON

FAWLEY
Village in Hampshire
- The Avon Arms

AVON COURT

MERIVALE PLACE
In Hampshire, some seven miles from Avon Court

~ | ~

" I have killed you! You are dead! You are dead!"
"You display an unseemly joy," he remarked. "I had no notion you were so bloodthirsty." — *Chapter XIII*

"*Voyons*, I have made you all laugh!" she said. "And I meant to make you laugh. I am a wit, *enfin!*"
— *These Old Shades*, Chapter XXIV

~ | ~

WHAT A QUIZ

Think you know your Heyer? These questions will test your knowledge...

1. In which year was *These Old Shades* first published?
2. What does Avon think is happening when he first meets Léon?
3. Who is married to Lady Fanny?
4. Who is king of France when the story takes place?
5. Name the king's famous mistress, mentioned in the book.
6. What are the nicknames that Rupert calls Léonie?
7. What name is shared by the sons of the Merivales and the Marlings?
8. What does Léonie call coffee?
9. Which prince wears Léonie's violets on his breast at Versailles?
10. What is Léonie's favourite expression?

ANSWERS: 1. 1926; 2. That his pocket is being picked; 3 Edward Marling; 4 Louis XV; 5. La Pompadour; 6. "wildcat", "spitfire"; 7. John; 8. pig-wash; 9. Condé; 10. "Bah!" (We will also accept "Lawks!").

~ | ~

WHAT THEY SAID

Contemporary Reviews of *These Old Shades*

Patronesses' Note: Oddly, especially given that her works had already received acclaim and were reviewed extensively by 1926, there are very few reviews of *These Old Shades* to be found from at the time it was published. Yet, it was an enormous success for Heyer, and would be her defining work for many years. What reviews there are extant are good ones, though.

The Sketch, November 17, 1926

Georgette Heyer is too modest in her title. The aristocratic fribbles of *These Old Shades* are alive, and lively, too, and their encounters and love affairs have none of the wistful ghostliness of Austin Dobson's eighteenth-century shades. The Court of Louis XV suits the English Duke of Avon very well, and his attendance at a Versailles levée has the authentic paint-and-powder charm. The satanic Duke picks up an orphan boy in Paris, being put on the alert by the child's likeness to his enemy, the Comte de Saint-Vire. It does not take him long (and it takes the reader no time at all) to discover that Leon is Leonie, nor that the Duke holds Saint-Vire, who has wickedly changed his daughter for a peasant's son at birth, in the hollow of his hand, so long as he has possession of Leon-Leonie. The little changeling is taken to England and taught to be a girl again, and the Duke turns out to be a susceptible and chivalrous Mephistopheles. *These Old Shades* is an excellent period piece, Miss Heyer has perceptibly advanced as a novelist since she wrote *Simon the Coldheart*.

~ | ~

The Daily Standard (Brisbane), December 11, 1926

LITERARY CONFECTIONARY

However sober people may be in their literary tastes, most of them turn at times from heavier mental food to the gay confectionery of romantic fiction. The daintiest of literary bon-bons is this story of the fashionable lords and ladies of France in the reign of Louis XIV., of a dissolute English duke, and of a red-headed page who alters the destiny of many people.

Justin Alastair, Duke of Avon, has reached the age of 40, with the nickname of "Satanas" and a vicious reputation as his sole gains. Squandering a fortune in his youth, he wins another at the gaming table, and gives himself over to self-indulgence, being connected with a succession of sordid scandals. His assets, if they may be considered, are good looks, intellect, and loyalty to the friends he chooses to keep.

For a whim he adopts a red-headed page, whom he discovers to be the daughter of his bitter enemy, de Saint Vire. Avon plans to use her as the instrument of his revenge, but Leonie, the page, has other views on the subject. For the first time the gay profligate finds himself an object of adoration, set upon a lofty pedestal of trust.

Life in sordid surroundings has not left Leonie untouched. She knows of Avon's reputation with women, yet is confident that he will never harm her. The cynical philanderer is disarmed by the Innocent audacity of a girl half his age, and after a series of exciting adventures Leonie becomes the Duchess of Avon. The story is told with a ready wit that makes bright reading.

~ | ~

SELECTED COVER GALLERY

Heinemann, UK
(1926)

Heinemann, UK
(1951)

Pan, UK
(1956)

Pan, UK
(1959)

Bantam, US
(1967)

Pan, UK
(1972)

Fawcett, US
(1979)

Signet, US
(1988)

Book of the Month Club
US (1992)

Arrow, UK
(2001)

ISIS Large Print, US
(2002)

Harlequin, Canada
(2003)

HQN, Canada
(2008)

Thorndike, UK
(2016)

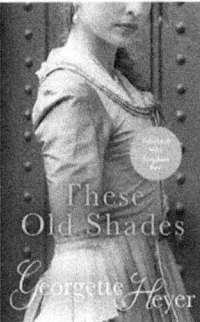
Cornerstone, UK
(2016)

SELECTED TRANSLATED EDITIONS

GERMAN: Rowohlt
(1964)

ITALIAN: Mondadori
(1972)

PORTUGUESE: Record
(1995)

HUNGARIAN: GABO
(2012)

ESTONIAN: Ajakirjade
(2016)

THESE OLD SHADES: A HISTORY BY JENNIFER KLOESTER

In 1922 a young Georgette Heyer began writing a new novel. She was nineteen and already had two published books under her belt. The first, *The Black Moth*, was a lively historical romance, and the second, *The Great Roxhythe*, was a much more serious novel set during the reign of King Charles II. The new manuscript was another historical novel originally intended as a sequel to The Black Moth. Georgette had recast the original villain of the piece, "Devil" Belmanoir, the Duke of Andover as the cynical, worldly-wise hero, Justin Alastair, Duke of Avon, also known as "Satanas". Despite his wicked reputation and sinful past Avon becomes hero and saviour of the young runaway, Léon/Léonie, and orchestrates a merciless revenge on the man who has deprived her of her birthright. Avon is not like most heroes: he is supremely confident, at times sinister, rich, powerful and practically omniscient. He minces into the story, clad in "purple satin, heavily laced with gold", grabs the reader by the throat and does not let go until the final page is turned. Even at nineteen, Georgette Heyer knew how to create a memorable character and set an intriguing scene.

She would eventually call her as-yet uncompleted novel *These Old Shades* – a direct reference to a line from the Victorian poet Henry Austin Dobson's "Epilogue" to his "Eighteenth Century Vignettes". The poem is a teasing commentary on the useful differences between contemporary and historical writing. In the former the author must be cognisant of modern-day scruples and trends; in the latter, the social and cultural mores of the period apply. As Georgette would discover, there was a decided advantage in being able to depict in a historical novel things that might have become distasteful or unacceptable in contemporary life. Things such as class and inherent snobbery, the power of kings and nobles, noblesse oblige, "buying a soul", and the idea that breeding will always tell, could all safely be used in an historical story, because those ideas "belonged to the past". She could also use real historical persons with impunity because such figures were long dead, and so King Louis XV, "La Pompadour", the Prince d'Armagnac, the Comte de Toulouse, the Gunning sisters, Horace Walpole, and many others could make their appearance in her story without its author suffering any "fear of defamation".

The title of the book is also a reference to the "shades" of some of Georgette's earlier characters who appeared in The Black Moth and whom she recast with new names and expanded roles. Frank Fortescue becomes Hugh Davenant, Lavinia Carstares becomes Fanny Marling, Richard Carstares becomes Edward Marling and Lord Andrew Belmanoir becomes Lord Rupert Alastair, while various minor characters also benefit from their transition from one book to the other. In one of her earliest known letters extant, the young Georgette told her agent that:

> "The sequel is naturally a much better book than The Moth itself, and is designed to catch the public's taste. I have also tried to arrange it that anyone who reads it need not first read The Moth. It deals with my priceless villain, and ends awfully happily.

This was January 1923 and the manuscript was nearly complete when, for some reason, Georgette put it aside. She published two novels that year: her only pseudonymous book, *The Transformation of Philip Jettan* (*Powder and Patch*) and her first contemporary novel, *Instead of the Thorn*. She wrote *Philip Jettan* in under three weeks and perhaps it was her familiarity with the scene and period which enabled her to write at such speed. The two novels are set about three years apart – *Philip Jettan* in approximately 1753 and *These Old Shades* in 1756 – and there are several elements common to both novels: the French Court, the magnificent costumes, the sprinkling of French throughout and the walk-on parts for real historical figures. There is also the "transformation" of the main character in each novel, although Philip's is very different from Léon/Léonie's. Where Philip must change from rustic boy to cultured man and his reason for doing so is his love for the fair Cleone, Léon's transformation is forced upon "him" by Avon who takes the runaway under his wing initially for revenge but ultimately because he comes to love the woman Léonie truly is. Avon's love proves to be unselfish: his original aim of using her to exact a vengeance forgotten as he comes to know and value the woman she is. His feelings for Léonie are new to him; they change him into a better man and though he is no less cynical, callous or sardonic with many people, with her he is a different person. It is this transformative power which also ties *The Black Moth* to *These Old Shades*.

In the first book, it is Devil Belmanoir's friend, Frank Fortescue, who, as the Duke says, "may Once More strive to direct mine Erring Footsteps on the Thorny Path to Virtue." In fact, Frank's wish for his erring friend is that he "might honestly fall in love – and that the lady might save you from yourself – my poor Devil!" In *These Old Shades* Avon's friend Hugh Davenant expresses a similar opinion when he tells Avon that the woman he failed to win, Jennifer Merivale, has "prepared the way for another woman to make you". It is Léonie who will "make" the Duke for she is unlike any woman he has ever known and it is her personality, intelligence, courage and capability that captivates not only Avon, but also the reader. Georgette describes her unusual heroine as having "*espièglerie*" – a roguish or frolicsome trait – but she is also an endearing combination of naiveté and worldliness with a "Puck-like quality of old and young wisdom". Léonie is Georgette Heyer's first "positive role model to a feminist critic".[1]

In this she is unlike the heroine of bestselling author Ethel M. Dell's 1922 novel, *Charles Rex*. Like *The Shepherd's Fairy*, one of Georgette's favourite childhood stories, *Charles Rex* was an obvious influence on *These Old Shades* and, though Dell's novel is contemporary and Georgette's historical, the two novels have many common elements: *Charles Rex* opens with the saving of Toby, a teenage "boy", from a beating; the saviour is an aristocrat, Lord Saltash; the boy is a nineteen-year-old girl, Nonette; she develops an unbreakable affection for her noble saviour; he takes her back to England and leaves her with friends to be cared for; "Toby" continues to wear breeches and becomes friends with her benefactress's brother, Bunny; Lord Saltash returns and tells her she must learn to be a girl; Nonette startles everyone when she appears as a beautiful girl dressed all in white; she loves Saltash and he loves her but neither understands how to communicate the true nature of their feelings until the end of the novel. Perhaps it was these obvious parallels which prompted Georgette to put her unfinished manuscript aside; we shall never know.

Some of the similarities between the two novels are unsurprising for they are common romantic tropes, while others seem proof conclusive that the teenage Georgette found in *Charles Rex* a useful foundation for her own novel. A few readers have concluded that the stories are similar enough to suggest plagiarism, however, this seems too strong a claim when one reads the books in parallel. Heyer's characterisation, dialogue and tone are very different from Dell's and there are major disparities between the books. Apart from the historical setting of *These Old Shades* and the book's far more vivid opening, Heyer's plot diverges from Dell's in a number of other important ways: there is no tale of revenge in Charles Rex; the story of Léonie's true birth, upon which so much of Georgette's story relies, is comprehensively told whereas Nonette's origins remain unimportant and untold until almost the end of the book; unlike Bunny, Rupert does not fall in love with Léonie nor offer her marriage; Avon does not marry Léonie before a mutual confession of love between them; Avon's friends and family support him in ways that Saltash's do not and there is no dramatic dénouement where the villain of the piece is revealed and socially disgraced – indeed, there is no villain in Dell's novel unless it be Saltash himself.

In their day, both novels proved hugely popular with readers but it is *These Old Shades* that has endured, remaining continuously in print since 1926, while Dell's audience began to diminish in the 1960s. *Charles Rex* remains an interesting read and the novel clearly played an important role in Georgette Heyer's early development as a writer. The success of *Charles Rex* was perhaps the reason behind Georgette's comment to her agent that she had 'packed [These Old Shades] full of incident and adventure, and have made my heroine masquerade as a boy for the first few chapters. This, I find, always attracts people!' Dell was not the only author to use the device, however, and Heyer would have been aware of Berta Ruck's 1923 bestseller, *Sir or Madam?* in which her heroine disguise herself as a male chauffeur, and Arthur Conan Doyle's *A Scandal in Bohemia* in which the remarkable Irene Adler confesses: "Male costume is nothing new to me. I often take advantage of the freedom which it gives." This is a sentiment echoed by Léonie in *These Old Shades* and several writers have commented on Heyer's repeated use of the cross-dressing plot device and its usefulness in enabling women to throw off the restraints endemic to their historical period.

Heyer's first biographer, Jane Aiken Hodge, described *These Old Shades* as 'compelling' and so it is. Even in these times of political correctness and cancel culture, the novel, for all its political incorrectness, continues to appeal to readers everywhere. Even at the young age of nineteen, Georgette Heyer knew how to create characters who leapt of the page and lodged themselves in their readers' minds, there to stay – often for a lifetime. As Hodge explained:

> It is easy to see why *These Old Shades* was an instant success. She was a compulsive writer and it is a compulsive read. Devil Andover from *The Black Moth* has suffered a seas change into the wicked Duke of Avon (known as Satanas to his friends). An older, saturnine hero with a past, he rescues a red-haired girl in boy's clothes from the Paris gutter, sets her up as his page, finally proves her aristocratic birth and marries her… There is high comedy too, some riveting scenes, and a mixture of tears and laughter that she would only sometimes achieve again. But the secret of the book's instant and lasting success lies in its sheer romantic gusto. She was writing with an easy pen that first year of her marriage.

Except she wasn't. Contrary to Hodge's assumption that all was well with Georgette and that her writing was once more flowing after her marriage in August 1925, this was far from true. Instead, she was still suffering from the death of her beloved father only two months earlier. His death caused in Heyer a grief so deep that she never fully recovered from it. It turned her inwards and stopped her from writing for two years. *These Old Shades* only came out in in 1926 because Georgette was contracted to Heinemann for a second book and, needing to fulfil her contractual obligations, she returned to her almost-complete manuscript, finished it and submitted it for publication. Hodge could not have known that she had already written most of These Old Shades, however, because the letters which would tell the real story would not come to light until 2001 – seventeen years after the publication of *The Private World of Georgette Heyer.*

The other myth attached to *These Old Shades* is that it came out during the General Strike and that, in spite of having no reviews or advertising, the novel sold 190,000 copies straight off the mark and made Georgette Heyer an instant bestseller. It is a wonderful story and has been repeated many times. Hodge states that:

> Georgette must have been writing *These Old Shades* at the time of her marriage in 1925, for it came out in 1926, during the General Strike when there were no trains, no newspapers and, of course, no advertising or reviews. An instant success, it sold 190,000 copies in hardback and established Georgette Heyer with a public and a publisher… The instant success of *These Old Shades*, without the benefit of publicity, may well have confirmed Georgette Heyer in her view that the public exposure she shrank from was unnecessary.

Instead, it was her father's unexpected death that prompted Georgette Heyer to choose privacy over publicity. Nor was *These Old Shades* published during the General Strike. The Strike happened in May 1926 and Heyer's novel appeared in October. It is true that it sold well from the first, however, and the novel had multiple printings in its first few years, but it is also true that it took more than ten years to reach the magical 190,000 copies sold. But whatever its success in 1926, it had little direct effect on Georgette, for in December she departed England and embarked on a voyage to Tanzania, there to meet Ronald who had gone out to Africa to prospect for tin.

However or whenever it was written, and regardless of its publication history, *These Old Shades* has nevertheless remained a firm favourite among readers for good reason: despite the romance and drama of the unlikely plot, the characters are completely convincing and their story utterly compelling.

– Jennifer Kloester

[1] Helen Hughes, "Georgette Heyer and the Changing Face of Historical Romance", essay, 1999.

~ | ~

"Dear Edward has given Fanny a chocolate-coloured coach with pale blue cushions. The wheat is picked out in blue." He held the sheet at arm's length. "It seems strange, but no doubt Fanny is right. I have not been in England for such a time... Ah, I beg her pardon. You will be relieved to hear, my dear Hugh, that the wheat still grows as it ever did. The wheels are picked out in blue."
— *These Old Shades*, Chapter VI

"I believe I have several times requested you not to call Rupert 'imbecile', infant."
"But Monseigneur, he is an imbecile!" she protested. "You know he is!"
"Undoubtedly, ma fille, but I do not tell the whole world so."
"Then I do not know what I am to call him."
— *These Old Shades*, Chapter XXIV

~ | ~

"Child, you do not know me. You have created a mythical being in my likeness whom you have set up as a god. It is not I. Many times, infant, I have told you that I am no hero, but I think you have not believed me. I tell you now that I am no fit mate for you. There are twenty years between us, and those years have not been well-spent by me. My reputation is damaged beyond repair, child. I come of vicious stock, and I have brought no honour to the name I bear. Do you know what men call me? I earned that nickname, child; I have even been proud of it. To no women have I been faithful; behind me lies scandal upon sordid scandal. I have wealth, but I squandered one fortune in my youth, and won my present fortune at play. You have seen perhaps the best of me; you have not seen the worst. Infant, you are worthy of a better husband. I would give you a boy who might come to you with a clean heart, not one who was bred up in vice from his cradle."

One large tear glistened on the end of her lashes.

"Ah, Monseigneur, you need not have told me this! I know—I have always known, and still I love you. I do not want a boy, I want only—Monseigneur."

"Léonie, you will do well to consider. You are not the first woman in my life."

She smiled through her tears.

"Monseigneur, I would so much rather be the last woman than the first," she said.

— *These Old Shades*, Chapter XXXI

~ | ~

THE WEEKLY POST, VOL I.
#1 - FINDING HEYER BY RACHEL HYLAND

Friday, July 3, 2020

It's such a common story that it almost amounts to cliché. I was eleven years old, it was the winter school holidays, and I had run out of books to read. I have always read widely, but my tastes then were largely confined to Enid Blyton boarding school stories, the continuing adventures of the Baby-Sitters Club, Greek Mythology, the Anne series, and frequent re-readings of *The Hobbit*.

I complained to my mother – herself an avid reader – of needing something new to delve into, and asked her to take me to our local library. Instead, she led me to the dark-panelled shelves which housed an enormous stockpile of paperbacks, and pointed me to a glassed-in section in which reposed dozens of well-loved, dogeared novels with evocative titles and white, heavily lined, spines.

"These are my Georgettes," she said. "Choose one."

I chose *The Convenient Marriage*, for what reason I cannot fathom – I do recall being quite taken with the cover, the gazebo in the background reminding me of the "You are sixteen, going on seventeen" scene from *The Sound of Music* – and while it has not remained a favourite, at the time it was the most incredible thing I had ever read. (*The Hobbit* notwithstanding.)

My mother would eventually go on to regret that early introduction to one of her favourite authors, I think, as I spent the next several months pretty much permanently locked in historical bliss, refusing to put my book (okay, her book) down for such mundanities as getting dressed, unstacking the dishwasher or entertaining my little brother. I was taken with the humour – though, of course, as time went by and I reread the novels again and again, I began to understand, and be amused by, ever more of it; Georgette Heyer is just like *The Simpsons* that way – and the romance. But more than anything I was taken with the immersion into a past reality. Yes, I had experienced such things when visiting Avonlea, not to mention *Little Women*, and *Treasure Island*, and my very beloved *Heidi*. But this was different. This was a grownup world into which I was being invited, like a debutante to her first ball, and I was thoroughly bewitched by the glitter and the glamour of it all.

Not much has changed in the decades since. If anything, my love of Heyer's work – well, *most* of her work, which will be discussed in greater detail over the ensuing weeks, months and even years to come – has only intensified. Which is but one reason of why these books have endured so long, and why Georgette Heyer (a rarity among so many of her contemporaries) continues to increase in popularity.

But the fact that she *was* increasing in popularity was something that all too many of us were unaware of for far too long, weren't we? Because Georgette Heyer is a name that is not nearly as widely known as it deserves to be – and that, our lovely members, is why we are all here.

The International Heyer Society is an undertaking that aims to promote the work of Georgette Heyer to readers all over the world. Not only do we want to join with those who already love her – as all here already do – but we also want to help foster her reputation as a writer of ineffable yet inestimable quality, and one whose legacy warrants more recognition throughout the literary world. Slowly, ever so slowly, her reputation is being redeemed from the depths of pulp romantic fiction where it has inexplicably lain for decades—but not fast enough for most of us. Not that there is *anything* wrong with pulp romantic fiction, I quite love that too, but for anyone who has read both, it is abundantly clear that there is no comparison. Mainly because Georgette Heyer is simply incomparable.

So, welcome to you all! Welcome to a fellowship of readers and enthusiasts who live and breathe Heyer's Regency (and Georgian period… and Medieval period… and contemporary early-1900s, etc.), and who want nothing more than to share their love with likeminded souls.

How did *you* come to Heyer? Share your tale with us, and (with your permission) we will feature it at the International Heyer Society website for your fellow members – and doubtless other Heyer readers around the world – to marvel at and/or relate to profoundly. Because the fact that we all found Heyer, and continue to adore her, is what we have in common… and is what makes us so unique, as well.

I look forward to getting to know you all better!

Yrs. affectionately,

Rachel Hyland, Patroness, the International Heyer Society

P.S. Thanks, Mum!

#2 - LADY JERSEY BY SUSANNAH FULLERTON

Friday, July 10, 2020

I was so honoured when Jennifer Kloester and Rachel Hyland invited me to be one of the Lady Patronesses of the new International Heyer Society. We each decided to take on the 'persona' of one of the real Lady Patronesses of Almack's, and I chose Lady Jersey. I earn my living giving talks, and Lady Jersey was such a great talker that she was given the nickname of 'Silence'.

Let me introduce you to this fascinating woman. Her name was Sarah (though she was usually called Sally) and her father John Fane, Earl of Westmorland, had eloped with her mother Sarah Child, only child of a fabulously wealthy banker. They were married at Gretna Green and in spite of the elopement, she inherited such a vast pile of blunt that she was one of the richest women in England. So Sally grew up in comfort and with huge expectations of wealth.

In 1804 she married George Villiers, 5th Earl of Jersey, in the drawing room of her Berkeley Square home. Sally's mother-in-law, the Countess of Jersey, had been one of the Prinny's mistresses, and she took many lovers throughout her married life. Sally's father-in-law was once asked why he'd never fought a duel over his wife's affairs, and he replied that this would have necessitated fighting every man in London!

Sally Jersey outlived her husband and six of her seven children. She was not an 'accredited beauty' but there are some rather wonderful portraits of her. In the one by Alfred Edward Chalon she wears a truly magnificent turban. Sarah also appears in a little illustration of dancing the Quadrille – it was she who introduced the dance, which had come from France, into Almack's in 1815.

Caroline Lamb ridiculed Lady Jersey in her novel *Glenarvon* which resulted in her being banned from Almack's, but Lady Jersey was a kind woman and after a while she rescinded the ban. She was noted for acts of generosity, was energetic and intelligent, and this is how she comes across in Georgette Heyer's novels. She was one of the most powerful of the Lady Patronesses and thus also had the title 'Queen Sarah'. Oh, what it must have been like to wield such social power!

She was noted for being strict about maintaining the exclusivity of Almack's. To get that coveted voucher, one had to dance well and obey the rules. In *Frederica* she refuses a voucher to arrogant Lady Buxted's very plain daughter, Jane – Lady Buxted had been rude to her in the past, yet is mortified when the voucher is refused.

She does, however, provide vouchers for the Merriville girls in *Frederica* and it is in that novel that she makes her fullest appearance. She arrives at Alverstoke's ball (both of them live in Berkeley Square) talking: "Lady Jersey was known, in certain circles, as Silence; but anyone who supposed that her flow of light, inconsequent chatter betokened an empty head much mistook the matter: she had a good deal of intelligence, and very little escaped her. She had been talking ever since she entered the room, and on an amazing number of subjects, ranging from the spate of nuptials imminent in the Royal Family to the escape of a gruesome murderer from the gallows, through the discovery of an ancient statute which allowed him to claim the right of wager by battle; but while she rattled on she had been taking mental notes, and very intriguing they were." As she talks, Lady Jersey manages to work out that Alverstoke is not seriously interested in Charis, that he is NOT giving the ball in honour of his niece Jane, and that his probable reason for the ball is to punish his sister, Lady Buxted. She also knows that Alverstoke has grown bored with his latest flirt. There are no flies on Lady Jersey, and it is clear that Alverstoke is fond of her. He even calls her 'my loved one' when he addresses her.

I hope as Lady Jersey, Patroness of this wonderful new society, I can exert kindly encouragement, bring pleasure through my invitations, and show a good understanding of our rules. I share Sally Jersey's love of talking. If only I could say that I too have an immense fortune, and Chalon to paint my portrait. Quite beyond my touch!

– Susannah Fullerton, Patroness, the International Heyer Society

#3 - LADY SEFTON BY JENNIFER KLOESTER

Friday, July 17, 2020

It is an honour to be a Patroness of the International Heyer Society and I am delighted to take on the persona of the admirable Lady Maria Sefton. Long renowned as one of the Patronesses of that most exclusive club, Almack's, Lady Sefton was regarded as the kindest of that cabal of formidable women. During the Regency Almack's seven Patronesses were Lady Jersey, Lady Cowper, Princess Esterhazy, Mrs Drummond-Burrell, Lady Castlereagh, Countess Lieven and Lady Sefton and it has been said that 'what the great clubs were to the men of the period, Almack's Assembly was to the whole of society, male and female.' These powerful ladies held high society in thrall with their coveted vouchers which were the only means of procuring a ticket of admission to London's most select club. So rigid were the rules of Almack's that even so great a personage as Duke of Wellington could be refused entry if he breached their rules. It was said that Lady Sefton preferred to stand apart when a person desiring a voucher was blackballed by the Patronesses.

Born Maria Margaret Craven on 26 April 1769, she was the daughter of the sixth Earl of Craven. On 1 January 1792 she married William Philip Molyneux, then Viscount Molyneux. In 1795, on the death of his father, he became the 2nd Earl of Sefton and Maria became a countess. The Seftons had four sons and six daughters and Lady Sefton outlived her husband by many years, dying on 1 January 1851. She and her husband were famous society hosts with a wide circle of friends among members of the aristocracy and Lady Sefton features in several of Georgette Heyer's Regency novels. In *Regency Buck*, the heroine, Judith Taverner, is told that 'Lady Sefton had to be liked also; and Mrs Scattergood assured her charges that neither she nor her popular husband had an enemy in the world.' It is Lady Sefton who comes forward to greet Judith at Almack's when both Countess Lieven and Princess Esterhazy stand aloof, and Lady Sefton who later introduces Judith to the Duke of Clarence after a church service at the Chapel Royal.

Lord and Lady Sefton were among Regency society's most powerful leaders: she as a Patroness Almack's and he as a member of the famous Bow-Window set. As one commentator wryly observed, 'I have never been sure who has the greater power in terms of keeping society in thrall to our whims and fancies.' The bow-window set was led by that *arbiter elegantiarum*, the great Beau Brummell. The Seftons were close friends of Brummell's and Lord Sefton was one of the small coterie of men allowed to sit in the bow-window of White's Club. Brummell had his appointed place there and would be joined by his friends to pass judgement on those walking past in St James's Street. It was later said that 'an ordinary frequenter of White's would as soon have thought of taking his seat on the throne in the House of Lords, as of appropriating one of the chairs in the bow-window.'

Like his wife, Lord Sefton was a genial man, with a lively sense of humour and a large circle of friends. He was a noted whip, a founding member of the Four-Horse-Club, Master of the Quorn from 1800-1805, and passionate about hunting, coursing, steeplechasing and racing. His love of fast driving earned him the humorous soubriquet, Lord Dashalong. He was also considered one of England's finest whist players but, like many of his peers at the time, he was an extravagant gambler and was said to have lost two hundred thousand pounds at Crockford's. When Beau Brummell eventually left England for Calais, there to live in relative penury until his unhappy death in an asylum, Lord Sefton was one of those who still continued to visit his old friend whenever he was in Calais.

Lady Sefton was a notable hostess and a charming guest. In *Arabella* she sends Lady Bridlington into transports when she attends the Bridlington's ball and speaks 'with the greatest kindness to Arabella, and had promised later on to send her a voucher admitting her to Almack's Assembly Rooms'. In *April Lady*, however, Heyer depicts her as having a lively curiosity when she visits Lady Letitia Merion in order to discover 'what truth there is in the rumours that are going about' about the Earl of Cardross's younger sister. But in her fleeting appearance in *Frederica* Lady Sefton smiles kindly on Endymion when he commits a social *faux pas* by ignoring her, while in *The Grand Sophy* she kindly escorts Sophy and her cousin Cecilia to Almack's when Cecilia's mama 'does not find herself equal to it this evening'.

When not in town the Seftons lived at Croxteth Hall, their country seat in West Derby near Liverpool in Lancashire. A grand house originally built in 1575, it would be home to the Molyneux family until 1972 when the last earl died and a worldwide search for an heir failed to find a successor to the estate. Maria, Lady Sefton was living there when the famous Liverpool Botanics was established in 1802 by William Roscoe in a walled garden on the estate. This remarkable horticultural collection is one of the oldest in Britain and was once world-famous for its collection of orchids. It was to Croxteth Hall that Sherry, Viscount Sheringham, travelled in *Friday's Child* in his desperate search for his missing wife, Hero, and it was at Croxteth that Lady Sefton 'dragged his story out of him' before 'favouring him' with a frank 'reading of his character'. Though generally kind, in this instance Lady Sefton 'reduced the unfortunate Viscount to the condition of speechless endurance to which she could, upon rare occasions, reduce her eldest born, my Lord Molyneux' before relenting enough to assure the hapless young husband that she would engage 'to smooth over any unpleasantness that might have arisen in influential quarters' over his wife's misdemeanour. In *Sylvester*, the heroine, Phoebe, is less enamoured of Lady Sefton after she attends the Sefton's ball and Lady Sefton introduces her to Sylvester as though she were 'conferring the greatest favour on me!' Perhaps because of this, Phoebe has no compunction in depicting Lady Sefton as the fictional Baroness Josceline – 'the affected, fidgety one' – in her novel, *The Lost Heir*. This clever *roman ã clef*, like the real book of the time, *Glenarvon* which was written by Lady Caroline Lamb, takes society by storm and eventually sees Phoebe at the centre of a social scandal.

For all that, Lady Sefton seems always to have been well-loved for her good-natured disposition and for being the most approachable of Almack's Patronesses I trust that I, too, will always be kind and amiable and generous in my role as Patroness of this wonderful new International Heyer Society.

– Jennifer Kloester, Patroness, the International Heyer Society

#4 - THE MAKING OF THE MOST EPIC (WELL, AT LEAST THE FIRST) GEORGETTE HEYER PODCAST! BY SARA-MAE TUSON

Friday, July 24, 2020

…Sounds awfully grandiose, doesn't it? It's a claim that's got the salty tang of hubris about it. Back when I first idly searched through my podcast app looking for a podcast reviewing Heyer's Regency work, almost five years ago now, I never would have dreamt that all these years later, I would have spoken or collaborated with more than 40 people, including actor Stephen Fry, written audio drama inspired by her letters, created original music for the score and gotten to know many experts on Heyer, who I now hope I can count as friends.

But that's how it all started. Me blinking myopically at my phone, stunned that this best-selling author, who has never been out of print, not only had almost no representations of her work on film (besides the one version of *The Reluctant Widow*, which Heyer famously disliked), yet even the medium which has something about everything, let me down.

Occupying what *Forbes* magazine calls a 'small part of the media stage' (garnering only 5% of ad revenue, compared to the larger shares of TV and radio), podcasts are still enjoying a major boom, drawing 100 million listeners per month. This, combined with the fact that the average audience listener age is 31 – "dramatically lower than its traditional media competitors' – means that, as a medium, 'it is building its foundations for the future."

But I wasn't to know that when I first invited my friend Beth to brainstorm with me about what a possible podcast about Heyer's work could sound like. All I knew was, I wanted to hear people talking about their love of her work. "There must be people like me out there, who want more Heyer content, right?"

Beth herself, though one of the most cultured and well-read people I know, had not encountered Heyer. Which led me to my next big idea. From the off, I hadn't wanted to do a standard, "two friends talking about books" podcast. There are already a proliferation of those, and my instinct with all my creative work is to find a fresh angle.

I'd already started developing *The Sugar Baby Confessionals*, which went on to win bronze at The British Podcast Awards in 2019, and Beth and I were very keen to make Fable Gazers, our little indie podcast company, stand out from the crowd as producers of unique, serial podcasts telling compelling (and hopefully evergreen) stories. I was keen to follow the examples of the journalistic podcasts I love most, like *Serial*, *Malcolm Gladwell's Revisionist Histories*, or *You Must Remember This*, by Karina Longworth.

"What if I try and convert other people to her work?"

"Hmm, risky," was Beth's response. Now, all these years later, I've released the first half of *Heyer Today*, and I've managed to cram into it my love of Heyer, as well as *all* my big ideas.

Over 26 episodes, we have interviews with celeb or expert fans, then biweekly book club episodes. In these, I try to convert people to one of her books (I kept the choices chronological, so I'd not be tempted just to put my favourite books in - I wanted to be fair, you understand, and give the listener an idea of the spectrum of quality of her work). We include a historical context segment where we look at what was going on in Heyer's life when she wrote each book. I wrote audio drama scenes, incorporating her actual words – culled from the letters Jennifer Kloester had so painstakingly sought out and dissected in her brilliant work, *Georgette Heyer: Biography of a Bestseller*.

A note about Jen, and Susannah Fullerton here. I could not have created this podcast without their help and boundless generosity. Jen's book brought me to tears by the end, because she'd managed to create such a living portrait of the woman I was trying to celebrate. Susannah, in turn, answered all my dumb questions and helped me get a sense of the sorts of people who might be willing to speak to me, most notably, Mr Stephen Fry, who'd written something for the accompanying pamphlet which went out to the attendees of the very first Georgette Heyer convention. I'm so grateful to these ladies and others of their ilk, kindred spirits like writers Joanne Harris, Garth Nix, Zen Cho, Harriet Evans, Emma Darwin and more, who allowed me to speak to them about Heyer.

Then there is the over-arching investigation (still ongoing), which is the thread holding the podcast together, drawing a narrative alongside the description of Heyer's life. In this thread, I explore why her books haven't been adapted for the screen in any meaningful way. When one considers the numerous Jane Austen adaptions (all of which I adore), you'd think Heyer would be a shoo-in, particularly in this 'golden age' of on-demand drama.

Of course, the pandemic has materially upended the film industry. Who can say what will be the result or when new projects, particularly expensive period shoots, will begin being made again? A part of me now thinks that, though it seemed like a Heyer telly series or movie seemed tantalisingly close, this terrible global turmoil will have pushed these plans back. I'll continue to investigate, however, because I really believe the hunger for her fans to see her work on their screens is there.

People always ask if I've made money from the podcasts I've created. The answer is, as for many other indie pods, no. Having done two crowdfunding campaigns, I've managed to get enough funds together to be able to work on these projects around other freelance editorial work, but in essence they've been a labour of love, the rewards of which, as only another true Heyerite can understand, are ephemeral. Most profoundly, I hope I'm creating something that other Heyer lovers will enjoy. So now, when someone scrolls through their podcast app looking for solace, they'll find other like-minded souls talking about Heyer in not one, but two Heyer podcasts (the excellent Georgette Heyer Podcast is now available too). So, if you need some post lockdown comfort listening, something which is very far removed from the horrors of the daily news, try this binge-worthy boxed-set for your ears, *Heyer Today*.

– *Sara-Mae Tuson, Guest Contributor*

#5 – COUNTESS LIEVEN BY RACHEL HYLAND

Friday, July 31, 2020

"It is a pity Countess Lieven wears skirts. She would have made an excellent diplomat."
– *Nicholas I, Tsar of Russia*

When our boundlessly clever Susannah Fullerton suggested that we Patronesses of the International Heyer Society each take on the persona of a different Almack's Patroness, I knew immediately which of those seven venerable ladies I would attempt to emulate: Dorothea, Countess Lieven. Not because I consider myself to be a diplomatic strategist of skill and renown, nor do I consider myself endowed with one tenth of her purported vivacity, intellect or fascination.

She's just my favourite.

Born Katharina Alexandra Dorothea Freiin von Benckendorff on December 17, 1785, in what is now Latvia, her father was a General and a Baron of German-Baltic ancestry, while her mother was a popular figure at the Romanov Court, as lady-in-waiting to Empress Maria, wife of Tsar Paul I. Dorothea, too, served the Empress, and, in 1800, at the age of just fourteen, she wed Count Christoph Heinrich von Lieven, twelve years her senior.

In 1809, the Count was sent to Berlin as ambassador to Prussia; then in 1812, in a particularly turbulent time, politically, between the British and Russian Empires, he was sent to London, where he served as Russian ambassador until 1834. Witty, intelligent, sophisticated and charming, Dorothea (whom, we must remember, was then only twenty-six years of age) quickly staked out a place at the very top echelons of English society, not only as the first foreign Patroness of Almack's – granting her privileges as arbiter of all that was fashionable, tonnish and respectable – but also as the mistress of some of the country's most powerful scions, from the Duke of Wellington to George IV himself. Indeed, her strategic liaisons were so plentiful – and all of them enabling her to build political influence and further the cause of Russia – that she could reasonably be said to have been the most powerful woman of the Regency era, and beyond.

What is perhaps most remarkable about the influence she wielded at the time is that the extent of it was not generally known. There were rumours of her cunning and her intrigues, of course, and she was famous for her friendships with many of the most distinguished men and women of the day, but it is only in examining the letters she left behind that historians and biographers have been able to put together a relatively complete picture of just how much she had to do with shaping the political landscape of early-19th century Europe.

In 1826, Count von Lieven's illustrious mother Charlotte, governess to the Romanov princes Nicholas and Mikhail, was granted the title of 1st Princess Lieven by the new Tsar Nicholas I – as she had previously been accorded that of 1st Countess Lieven, in 1799 – and as a result, the younger Lievens began to style themselves as Prince and Princess, which was their right. I remember being shocked when I learned this piece of trivia some years ago, researching an unrelated topic, as I had always simply assumed that it was through his own offices, or even those of his wife, that the ambassador of whom I tangentially knew (it is notable that Countess Lieven makes frequent appearances in Regency-set literature, but the Count rarely appears) rose in the ranks. Not so. It was all his because of his mum.

In 1834, when Prince Lieven was recalled to St. Petersburg, Dorothea was devastated to leave behind her life of social supremacy in London. She and the Prince, with whom she had six children – one daughter and five sons, only two of whom survived her – had dealt together quite amicably across the decades, presenting a united front in public while carrying on multiple and often advantageous affairs in private, but the move back to Russia did not suit Dorothea at all. Before long she had abandoned the Imperial Court for Paris, where she established herself once more as a leader of society, and became embroiled again in high-level diplomacy. She fell in love there with statesman François Guizot, and when he was appointed French ambassador to Britain in 1840, she accompanied him to London. By then, the Prince had died, but she and Guizot never married, a circumstance that has puzzled historians and biographers to this day – but which I speculate was simply because she didn't want to give up her exalted title. The pair stayed together for the rest of her life, however, publicly living apart but always in each other's company, as well as exchanging over five thousand letters imbued with much love and, of course, politics.

Princess Lieven died, with Guizot and her son Paul at her bedside, in 1857, at the age of 71.

In the world of Georgette Heyer, Countess Lieven appears in several novels, sometimes in passing, at others positively stealing the scene with her Eustacie de Vauban-like *patois*. In *Frederica* she is described as "haughty" and "malicious" – but the latter is when dealing with Lady Buxted, so that's okay – and *April Lady*'s Nell Cardross calls her "odious," but since I dislike the drippy Nell almost as much as I do her lord, I have felt comfortable discounting her opinion entirely.

But it was in *The Grand Sophy* in which I fell in love with the Countess Lieven, when our Sophy gallops – *gasp!* – her horse – *gasp!* – in Hyde Park – *gasp!* – and is taken to task for her want of conduct by the very superior Miss Eugenia Wraxton. Just as the peril of this wantonness, and how she might now be – *gasp!* – excluded from Almack's, is being painstakingly explained to her, Sophy notes the arrival of "Madam de Lieven" upon the scene... who is enchanted to see Sophy, makes mention of two other Patronesses who will be just as happy, promises her a voucher to Almack's, and does no more than gently chide her for riding *ventre á terre*.

Not only was it the glorious patroness *ex machina* of the scene that awoke my interest in this great lady, but also Sophy's description of her: "... she is clever, and can be amusing."

I would like that to be my epitaph.

– *Rachel Hyland, Patroness, the International Heyer Society*

#6 – TOURING WITH GEORGETTE HEYER BY SUSANNAH FULLERTON

Friday, August 7, 2020

Many years ago, on a visit to London, I did a self-guided walk to see places connected with Georgette Heyer. It was so special to stand in front of the Albany, to stroll past the statue of Beau Brummell and remember Judith's meeting with him, to see where Almack's was situated and think of those hallowed doors through which so many of her characters long to pass.

I should have been in London earlier this year, leading one of my literary tours, but Covid meant that was not possible and so I was not able to wander along St James's, or pause in Berkeley Square and wonder which house could have been the residence of the Marquis of Alverstoke. As I have been unable to give my usual talks on authors and their works during recent months, I've been keeping busy by creating virtual or video talks. These are about an hour each, and take people travelling, through my recorded commentary and lots of fabulous images, to places of literary interest. I've now created talks on Jane Austen and her novels, Louisa May Alcott and *Little Women*, Thomas Hardy and *Tess of the D'Urbervilles*, Anthony Trollope and *Barchester Towers*, and then two travel talks on my Top Ten Places in Literary England and in Literary Scandinavia.

I then decided the time had come to create a talk on Georgette's fabulous historical world, to see how places had changed since the Regency – what was still there and what had disappeared through development – and which places in London and throughout England she uses most often as settings. Do you know which county comes up most often as a setting in her books? Which characters go to Bath, and where they stay when they get there; who visits Cheltenham, or Newmarket, or Brighton? My talk provides a brief overview of Georgette's life (if you want lots of fabulous detail, then go to Jennifer Kloester's biography) and then takes you travelling from the gentlemen's clubs in London to the Brighton Pavilion.

Georgette Heyer was intensely aware of the importance of location and she researched places scrupulously. I learned new things about Georgette and her superb craftsmanship while preparing this illustrated talk – I hope you will learn new things from it too. It was such a pleasure to create this tribute to an author whose novels have given me such enduring pleasure. I've included a guide to further reading at the end, in case you want to explore her world in greater detail.

I hope you will come with me on this virtual journey through a fictional world we all love and celebrate the artistry and brilliance of the fabulous Georgette!

– *Susannah Fullerton, Patroness, the International Heyer Society*

#7 – MAYFAIR PET ADOPTION AGENCY BY RACHEL GRANT

Friday, August 14, 2020

Charming Pets for the Upper Ten Thousand
New Listings this week:

LUFRA

- A large, shaggy pure-bred Baluchistan Hound. These dogs are very rare and are famous for their fidelity, especially when untainted by any Barcelona Collie genes.
- Not fierce or savage, but can be over-friendly to small children.
- May "forget himself" amongst cows and other livestock.
- Dislikes: being "bundled" into carriages.
- Would suit a large, lively family living on a country estate, as he finds city parks confining.

IN A WORD: Loyal

ULYSSES

- Small and sandy-coated Crossbreed. He is a rare specimen and his family tree would surprise you. He is not at all like sporting dogs.
- Can be reduced to blissful idiocy by having his ears scratched.
- Particularly likes loin chops and travelling in carriages, in fact he was born to be a Carriage Dog.
- Dislikes: Poodles
- His sores are healing nicely and he would make a devoted companion for a strong-willed Gentleman who can keep Ulysses' vulgarian habits in check.

IN A WORD: Toadeater

FLURRY

- An amiable, if somewhat vacuous Spaniel, with an excitable disposition.
- Incurably gun-shy, but is much addicted to the sport of chasing rabbits and flushing pheasants.
- Flurry will "sit" when commanded but spends a lot of his time gambolling about in the undergrowth, which makes him a poor escort for a lady.
- Suffers mental perturbation frequently.
- Would suit a patient owner.

IN A WORD: Idiotish

BOUNCER

- A large, young Hound, barely out of puppyhood, with teeth in excellent condition.
- Bouncer likes hunting and is nearly trained not to kill chickens or chase sheep.
- He takes a benevolent interest in cats, livestock and stray visitors.
- Particularly enjoys a good marrow or ham bone although would never touch food from a stranger.
- Shows excellent promise as a guard dog.
- Dislikes: Flea-ridden terriers.
- Would suit a young, energetic Gentleman who likes to stride out over the estate, or hack through the countryside on a prime thoroughbred.

IN A WORD: Chaos

PUG

- An elderly, snorting Pug dog with a wheezy bark
- Has a lethargic disposition and is overfed and over-indulged.
- Dislikes: being thrust into travelling carriages when out for his evening waddle.
- Would suit an elderly or indolent Peeress of the Realm, or someone who has plenty of servants or young ladies at her beck & call, to take Pug out on his leash.

IN A WORD: Stertorous

– Rachel Grant, Animal Correspondent

#8 – IN PURSUIT OF THE DUST JACKET OF *THE BLACK MOTH* BY PROFESSOR CHRIS BROWNE

Friday, August 21, 2020

As a serious book collector, I am always trying to find copies of significant books in the best possible condition. I generally try to collect the first British editions of British books in their original binding and complete with the original dust jacket wherever possible. However, I do sometimes stray, and collect the first British editions of American authors as well as the first US edition of British authors.

As you will know from the first issue of *Nonpareil* as well as perhaps from Jennifer Kloester's excellent biography *Georgette Heyer* (Heinemann, 2011), Heyer's first book was *The Black Moth*, written when she was only seventeen and published when she was barely nineteen in London by Constable in September 1921. Jennifer Kloester shows a picture of the top cover of the binding of that edition in her book. However, the dust jacket of this book is essentially unknown. It was the sad fashion in the 1920s and 1930s for people to remove and discard dust jackets from their books, so there are many instances of novels from that period where the first edition of the book is not particularly scarce but the dust jacket is effectively unobtainable.

I don't have a copy of the first impression of the first British edition of *The Black Moth* in my collection, but I do have a copy of the second impression, published in 1922, as well as a copy of the first impression of the first US edition that was published in November 1921 by Houghton Mifflin in New York. Neither books have their original dust jackets.

This first American edition of *The Black Moth* is bound in black cloth, just like the first UK edition, shown in Jennifer Kloester's book. Interestingly, my copy of the UK second impression is bound in a deep red cloth. The title page of my Constable edition has no date on it, unlike the American edition, but on the back (or *verso* as it is properly called) of the title page, you will find two printed lines: *"First Published - 1921"* followed by *"Second Impression 1922"*. Both my Houghton Mifflin and Constable editions have the same dedication printed on the page opposite the title page, where you can see "To G.B.H.", which refers to George Boris Heyer, Georgette's brother.

The Houghton Mifflin edition of *The Black Moth* has a text block of 334 pages, which is the same as my Constable edition from London. This is no great surprise, as the American edition was made up from pages printed in the UK for Constable that were sent over to the USA for binding. Both books have the same printer's name printed on the penultimate end paper, where you can read *"Printed in Great Britain by the "Hampshire Advertiser" Co., Ltd., Southampton."* on my Constable second impression and *"Printed by the "Hampshire Advertiser" Co., Ltd., Southampton."* on the Houghton Mifflin American edition.

Both bindings are in cloth with the title and author's name on what normal people call the front and the spine, but what we book collectors call the "top board" and the "back-strip". However, there are some differences, as both the text and font used for the words printed on the bindings are different. Where the UK binding uses an all upper-case font with dots between the words, the American binding uses a lower case font with some upper case initial letters for the title, and in addition the subtitle "A Romance of the 18th Century" appears on the title page, the top board and the back-strip of the American edition, where it only appears on the title page in the Constable editions. The word "By" also precedes the author's name on the American binding.

It must be noted that the binding of my Constable second UK impression differs from the UK and American first editions in the colour of the book cloth, red rather than black, and the addition of a graphical device or colophon of a lamp and the words *Ex Libris* in the centre of the top board.

All of this reinforces that the Constable binding was designed and made in the UK, whereas the Houghton Mifflin binding was designed and made in the USA, by someone who must have seen the original UK binding of the first Constable edition.

Intriguingly, although my 1921 and 1922 copies of *The Black Moth* lack the original dust jackets, my American edition has a "made-up" dust jacket which is clearly a colour photocopy of the binding. You can tell this easily as some of the small blemishes on the binding reoccur on the dust jacket.

This leads me to speculate that perhaps the original, now lost, dust jacket was the same design as the binding. A largely black dust wrapper would be appropriate for a book with the word "Black" in its title, and I do have a few instances in my collection of American bindings and dust jackets of the right period that are identical. Perhaps the unknown person who made the photocopied dust jacket had seen a real original American dust jacket for *The Black Moth*.

If my speculation is correct, then perhaps the original British dust jacket from September 1921 was a copy of the Constable binding, as the American designer of the binding was clearly copying the British design. It also makes me wonder whether the dust jackets of the UK first and second impressions are identical, give the small differences in the binding design and the different coloured cloth.

However, unless the original dust jackets of these almost 100-year-old books turn up one day, we shall probably never know.

– Professor Chris Browne, Special Contributor

#9 – THE TRANSFORMATION OF PHILIP JETTAN: THE FINAL CHAPTER

Friday, August 28, 2020

In April of 1923, Mills & Boon published *The Transformation of Philip Jettan* by Stella Martin. In March of 1930, Heinemann published *Powder and Patch* by Georgette Heyer. Despite the two different author names, the two novels were the same book – with just one difference. In its second publication under her real name, Georgette had agreed to discard the original final chapter.

The question is: why?

In the years between the two publications, Heyer had written four contemporary novels and four more historical novels. In that time she had learned a lot and her skill had inevitably improved; on reading the two endings it is easy to see that the final paragraphs of the original penultimate chapter is the kind of ending that she would come to write in future books where Heyer leaves the hero and heroine's life after marriage to the reader's imagination. In the 1923 version of *Philip Jettan* the original final chapter shows us Philip and Cleone in Paris making their debut as married couple. The reader sees something of their relationship and its synergy but not enough to really know whether these two will grow together or apart; there is not the space in a single chapter for a developed relationship. It is only in later novels where the protagonists are married early on that Heyer focuses the gradual development of mutual friendship, love and understanding.

In her excellent biography, *The Private World of Georgette Heyer*, Jane Aiken Hodge astutely observed that by deleting the last chapter Heyer 'totally chang[ed] the emphasis of the book'. This is true and it seems likely that, eight years after writing it, Heyer realised that the Paris chapter gave a very different impression of Philip and Cleone's relationship than the one we see at the end of the second-last chapter. In deleting the Paris episode, she gave her readers the requisite happy ending and one which did not raise questions about her happy couple's likely future: England or

France? Exquisites or a country gentleman and his wife?

There is one other point that may have clinched her decision to delete: the closing line of original *Philip Jettan* is in French. Perhaps, by 1930, Heyer had decided that this was not the ideal ending for her readers – that it assumed too much about their education and taste and was better left out. Certainly, the removal of the original final chapter does not detract from the fun or the romance of the novel and having both versions is like having two different kinds of delicious desserts from which to partake.

– Jennifer Kloester, Patroness, the International Heyer Society

Here, just in case you haven't yet encountered it, we present that original final chapter, in full.

Chapter XX

Mademoiselle de Chaucheron Rings Down the Curtain

SIR MAURICE JETTAN stood in the withdrawing-room of the Hotel Cleone and studied himself in the glass. He smiled a little, and straightened his shoulders.

There came a swish of skirts in the passage without, and the door opened. In walked Cleone, a fair vision in a gown of pure white satin and lace.

Sir Maurice turned. He raised his quizzing-glass the better to inspect his daughter-in-law.

"Upon my soul, Cleone!" he ejaculated.

Cleone swept him a curtsey, laughing.

"Is it not ridiculous? Philip insisted. Wait till you see him!" She ran to the mirror. "Do you like the way my hair is dressed, father?"

"I am struck dumb by the whole effect!" answered Sir Maurice. "Yes, I like that white rose in your hair."

"Oh, you must tell Philip that! He spent hours and hours trying to place it to his entire satisfaction! It has been terrible, *je t'assure*. Yes, I am beginning to acquire an accent, am I not? Philip nearly tore his beautiful wig in his anxiety!" She re-arranged the roses at her breast. "At one time I expected him to summon François to his assistance. But he refrained, and here am I!"

Sir Maurice sat down.

"Has he been dressing you, my dear?"

"Has he—! For the past three hours, sir! He has driven my maid distracted." She started to count on her fingers. "He spent half an hour superintending my hair-dressing, and another half an hour placing this rose, and the pearls. Then half an hour went to my patches – this is when he nearly tore his wig! – he could not decide where to put them. The arrangement of my gown occupied quite an hour in all. And then he was much put out over my jewels." She held up her fingers. "I vow they are red and sore, sir! I have had rings pushed on them, and dragged off them, until I was nigh screaming with impatience! But now I am dressed – and I have been told on pain of Philip's direst wrath to *n'y toucher pas!*" She sat down on the couch beside Sir Maurice, and slipped her hand in his. "Is he not absurd? And oh, I am prodigious nervous!"

"Why, my dear? What should make you so?"

"You see, it is my first appearance in Paris – it is to be my first ball – and I am so afraid I shall not understand what is said to me, or – or something mortifying!"

"Not understand? Nonsense, Clo! Why, you have talked hardly any English since you have been married."

"Y-es, but I am not at all fluent. Philip says everyone will be most amiable, but – oh, dear!"

At that moment François darted into the room, a harassed frown on his face.

"Ah, *pardon, madame! Pardon, m'sieu! Je cherche la tabatiere de m'sieu' Philippe!*"

"Laquelle?" asked Cleone. Sir Maurice was amused by her serious air. "The one with the pearls?"

"*Mais oui, madame*. It is this fool of a Jacques who has lost it, *sans doute! Ah, la voilà!*" He seized the errant box and skipped out again. Cleone breathed a sigh of relief.

"How terrible if it had been really lost!" she said.

Sir Maurice laughed.

"Would it have been so great a catastrophe?"

"But of course! It matches his dress, you understand."

"I see." Sir Maurice smothered another laugh. "My dear, do you know that it is three years since last I was in this city of cities?"

"Is it? Don't you think it is a wonderful place? Philip took me for a walk yesterday, and I was enchanted! And this house – I know I shall never bear to leave it! Philip says that the Hotel Cléone will be the most fashionable one in Paris! I was so surprised when he brought me here! I had no idea that there was a house waiting for me. He and François got all ready the week before our marriage! I've never been so happy in my life! And to-night I am to see Philip in what he calls his *milieu*. He tells me he was never at home in London."

"Philip in his *milieu*. Paris." Sir Maurice smiled down at her. "When I think of what Philip was not quite a year ago…"

"It seems impossible, doesn't it? But oh, I am glad now that I sent him away. He is quite, quite perfect!"

"H'm!" said Sir Maurice.

Cleone laughed at him.

"You pretend! I know how proud you are!"

"Minx! I confess I am curious to see Philip in his Parisian Society. No one knows that he is here?"

"Not a soul. He insisted on guarding the secret until he could make a really dramatic appearance at the Duchesse de Sauverin's ball to-night. He is mad, you know, quite mad! Oh, here he is!"

Philip came into the room with a rustle of stiff silks. Sir Maurice started at him.

"Good God, Philip, what audacity!"

From head to foot his son was clad in white. The only splash of colour was the red heels of his shows; his only jewels were pearls and diamonds; on the lapel of his coat he wore a single white rose.

"Isn't it ridiculous?" said Cleone. "But doesn't he look beautiful?"

"Stand up, child, and let me see you side by side… Yes. What audacity! Had I known, I would have attired myself in black – the old man at the ball."

"Twould have made an excellent foil," agreed Philip. "But no matter. Cleone, you have rearranged your roses!"

Cleone backed, warding him off.

"I cry your pardon, sir! Oh no, let me be!"

Philip came to her, and with deft fingers pulled the flowers into position.

"One of them must kiss your skin, so! To show that it is no whiter than the skin. *Voilà, c'est bien!*"

"Who is like to be at the ball to-night, Philip?" asked his father.

"*Tout le monde*. One always goes to Madame de Sauverin's balls. It is *de rigueur*."

"We shall be late!" warned Cleone. "Oh, we are late now!"

"That is also *de rigueur*," said Philip.

*　　*　　*　　*　　*

"Sir Maurice, *M'sieu'*, *et Madame* Jettan!!" announced the lackey.

There was a sudden hush. All eyes turned to the late-comers. In the doorway stood a tall gentleman, at his side two dazzling visions in white.

Madame de Sauverin stared for a moment in wonderment. Then she hurried forward, hands outstretched.

"Philippe!"

"Philippe! *Le petit* Philippe!" A score of voices took up the cry. Nearly everyone there surged forward.

Philip kissed Madame's hand.

"*Chere madame!* I may present my wife? My father you know."

Cleone curtseyed low.

"Your – wife!" Madame took Cleone's hands. "*Voyons, voyons, notre petit Philippe s'est éspousé! Et Maurice!*"

Philip and Cleone were at the centre of a welcoming throng. Cleone's hand was kissed a dozen times, delighted questions were shot at Philip.

Saint-Dantin grasped his hand.

"*Mon cher petit!* You have returned at last? *Et madame!*" He bowed to the blushing Cleone. "There is no need to ask who is madame." He smiled at her. "It is evident that her name is – Cléone!"

De Vangrisse pressed forward.

"The mysterious Cléone! Madame, *votre serviteur!* We have all longed to see the lady who so consistently held Philip's while heart!"

"Philippe, how long have you been in Paris?" demanded De Chatelin. "You are going to remain? *Ah bon!*"

"Philippe, have you an ode for the occasion?" asked another laughing voice.

Clothilde de Chaucheron pushed through the ring.

"*Le petit Philippe au cœur perdu!*" she cried.

Philip disengaged himself from the clutches of Saint-Dantin and took his wife's hand.

"Mademoiselle de Chaucheron, *chérie*," he said, and bowed.

Clothilde gazed at Cleone for a moment. Then she swept a deep curtsey.

"*Je me trompe,*" she said, smiling. "*Le petit Philippe au cœur trouvé.*"

THE END

AND NOW FOR A TRANSLATION…

Unlike Georgette Heyer, most of us are not proficient French speakers, which is very much what she seemed to expect of us throughout this book. (And several more besides this one, but most especially in this one.) Now, the English and French languages have enough in common that we poor monolinguists can often get the gist of what is going on from context clues and the occasional semantic similarity, but there are times where a little explicitness does not go astray.

Here, Mademoiselle de Chaucheron's final pronouncement may require a little clarity for the non-Francophile. If you will recall, she, and much of fashionable Paris, had taken to calling Philip "Little Philip without a heart" (this translation courtesy of Sir Maurice) – or even possibly "Little Philip of the lost heart," which makes more sense – because he would obstinately insist on *not* falling in love with any of the Parisian women he so captivated, instead remaining obsessed by Cleone. Clothilde greets him as such, but at the sight of his new bride, changes her mind and says:

> "*I am wrong. Little Philip has found his heart.*"

Sweet, right? Especially when you can understand it.

– Rachel Hyland, Patroness, the International Heyer Society

#10 – A MATTER OF URGENCY BY SUSANNAH FULLERTON

Friday, September 4, 2020

Where did a lady such as Arabella or Sophy or Nell go, when she really needed to go? Finding toilets when out in public is not a problem discussed by Georgette Heyer in her novels, but it is interesting to think about how men and women managed when too much tea had been drunk, or the wine had been flowing freely.

At home in Yorkshire, at her father's rectory, Arabella would have been able to make use of a chamber pot in her room, or a 'necessary' or earth closet somewhere in the garden. I have heard that such earth closets often had roses planted around the door to help lessen nasty odours, and that this gave rise to the euphemism of 'going to smell the roses' when one needed the toilet, but I have not been able to verify that story. I'd love to know if you have more information on this anecdote?

However, it was a different matter when a lady was in London or Bath and attending balls or church services. What did one do if feeling seriously uncomfortable? Well, there was a useful little device that one's abigail could discreetly carry and have at hand when required. This was a bourdaloue, a small and compact vessel that came with a cover and in shape looked rather like a modern gravy boat. The edges were rounded and turned inwards, so there would be no danger of injury to softer parts of the anatomy. One's abigail could hand over the bourdaloue and, once a private corner had been located, a lady could use the device while standing up. The maid would then need to find somewhere to empty the bourdaloue after use.

It is not known exactly how this useful device came to be so named. Louis Bourdaloue was a Jesuit priest who lived from 1632 to 1704. His sermons were evidently very long. According to one story, his female parishioners were so entranced that they did not wish to lose a word he uttered, so discreetly used the bourdaloue while in a church pew. The other tale goes that his sermons were so terribly long that one needed to find some relief when it would have appeared rude to leave the church. Artist François Boucher did a rather fabulous painting of an 18th century French lady making use of her bourdaloue, but she is in a house, not a church. There is also speculation that the word 'loo' comes from the priest's name, but again I have no verification of this.

I find it very hard to picture Nell Cardross, attending the Chapel Royal, needing to make use of the device, with all the resulting sound effects that must have been involved, and then having to give her maid Sutton the task of disposing of the vessel's contents.

Surviving bourdaloues are very attractive. Made of porcelain or faience, they are prettily painted with flowers and landscapes. They would be useful for taking on a long coach journey, or to the theatre (which had no public conveniences). When they first came into use in Georgian Britain, women had very full skirts and petticoats – it was easy to hide and use the little vessels under voluminous clothing. But even when dresses were of light muslin and more classical lines were introduced into women's clothing during the Regency, the device was too useful to give up. Georgette's heroines would just have needed to find some private spot in which to make use of their bourdaloues. They remained in use until well into the Victorian period.

For any of Georgette's heroines visiting Vauxhall Gardens and finding that the famous rack punch, or the ratafia they had drunk was passing rather too rapidly through the system, there was a ladies' cloakroom they could visit. This was depicted by illustrator Samuel William Fores but it does not show any form of toilet that could be used, so perhaps ladies all brought out their bourdaloues once there? I suspect that most ladies going out into public monitored their liquid intake very carefully, knowing that going to the toilet was not always possible or convenient.

Gentlemen have always had it easier when it comes to finding bladder relief. At Vauxhall it was simple for a man to nip behind a handy bush (whereas women could be at risk in venturing into darker parts of the gardens). And when dining out, men didn't even need to leave the room – a chamber pot tucked into a dresser cupboard could be used as soon as the ladies withdrew from the room. An 1816 print held by the Fitzwilliam Museum depicts an obviously 'foxed' gentleman attempting to make use of the chamber pot, and missing! I have also heard of chamber pots being placed behind dining room screens, so that those in need during dinner could simply retire behind the screen for a few moments. But there would have been no sound-proofing and again I find it very hard to imagine the Grand Sophy or prim Eugenia Wraxton resorting to such an expedient.

Drawers, or some form of underpants, were starting to become the norm by the Regency period. Women of the older generation (Arabella's godmother, for instance) are most unlikely to have worn any undergarment except for a shift, but by about 1830 underpants were becoming standard wear and this would have made using a bourdaloue a little more challenging. So, the Regency was a time of change in this respect, and it was up to each individual woman to decide what she could afford and what made her most comfortable.

Disposing of human waste was something of a problem for any Regency household. Amazingly, a form of flush toilet was available to Queen Elizabeth I, and the S-trap, a crucial advance in plumbing, was invented by a Scotsman in 1775. In 1771 a patent was taken out for a 'plunger closet'. An inventor called Joseph Bramah made toilets for London homes from his business premises in St Giles, but it was only a few decades after the Regency era that flush toilets became widely used and marketed in Britain.

Perhaps the people of the Regency were less private and less squeamish about such matters than we are today. The gutters must often have been full of human and animal waste, and bad smells were taken for granted in their environment. When reading Georgette Heyer's fabulous novels, we tend to see only the elegant side of Regency life and forget the smells, unpleasant sights and how awful it must have been to live without modern sewage. I hope I have not lowered the tone of our august Heyer Society with this article, but hope you have found it interesting to learn more about a very necessary activity, not only of the Regency, but of any era.

– Susannah Fullerton, Patroness, the International Heyer Society

#11 – YOU'RE MUCH TOO YOUNG, GIRL BY CLARA SHIPMAN

Friday, September 11, 2020

When I was a teenager, I was obsessed with *Twilight*. In my defense, it was the 2000s and *Twilight* obsession was everywhere and was hardly confined to teens. But I would say I was fairly hardcore, even in the realms of (I hate this term) Twi-hards—I read the books repeatedly and bought all the merchandise, posted online pretty much hourly with my fellow obsessives and saw the first couple of movies multiple times in the theater, on the same day.

One thing that I used to find so infuriating back then was that people were always accusing Edward Cullen, a 100+ year old vampire and my ideal man, of child sex offences, because love of his life Bella Swan is only 17. It seemed to me so unfair, not only because I didn't think that Edward would have been taking advantage of *me* if we met and fell in love, and I was younger than Bella (there may even still be fanfic about that possibility somewhere), but because those same people didn't seem to give the 200+ vampire Angel the same level of grief over *his* 16-year-old girlfriend, Buffy. (Was it because she was good with a stake? Probably.)

Sometime during this period, my Grandmother introduced me to Georgette Heyer, intending, she later confessed, to wean me off the "sparkly vampire books" and get me into reading "decent literature." She gave me *The Black Moth*, and I was into it right away. Before long, I had lessened my time spent on Edward, Bella and the gang – I didn't even see *The Twilight Saga: Breaking Dawn, Part 1* in theaters until it had been out for over a week (!!!) – and was devouring Heyer novels, one after the other, for at least the next year.

And one thing I kept noticing, as I continued through the catalog, was just how many of these romances were taking place between people of vastly different ages and levels of experience. It wasn't just that the women were virginal, because they were unmarried and so had to be (Edward would approve), it was that they were very often *so much younger* than the men they ended up marrying. Sometimes worryingly so.

And sometimes, it wasn't even the age *difference* that concerned me, but the age itself. It was one thing, I felt, for Bella to find her true love at 17, get married at 18 and settle down to an eternity with Edward and their freaky speed-growing baby. It was another for girls even younger to be locking themselves into marriage, and in a time when there was no such thing as a quickie divorce and they *weren't* being turned into forever-young vampires.

Horry in *The Convenient Marriage* is 17 when she offers herself up to the Earl of Rule, in place of her beautiful older sister whose heart lies with another. 17 and married! To a man of 35, eighteen years her senior.

The Corinthian's runaway Pen is likewise 17 when she falls into the arms of Sir Richard Wyndham, 29 and far more worldly than the sheltered, naïve Pen. And sure, he *says* he's not interested:

> "Rid yourself of the notion that I cherish any villainous designs upon your person," he said. "I imagine I might well be your father. How old are you?"
> "I am turned seventeen."
> "Well, I am nearly thirty," said Sir Richard.
> Miss Creed worked this out. "You couldn't possibly be my father!"
> "I am far too drunk to solve arithmetical problems. Let it suffice that I have not the slightest intention of making love to you."

But by the end of the book, he definitely does, despite her years.

And Hero! In *Friday's Child*, she really is one, still sixteen when she marries the 23-year-old Lord Sheringham (he, out of spite; she, out of hero worship and desperation). And she was definitely not ready for adulthood, let alone marriage, at all:

> Within a month of their taking up their residence in Half Moon Street, it had been borne in upon his lordship that his wife was no more fit to carve her way through life than the kitten he called her. His lordship, who had never known responsibility, or shown the least ability to regulate his own career on respectable lines, found himself sole lord and master of a confiding little creature who placed implicit faith in his judgement, and relied upon him not only to guide her footsteps, but to rescue her from the consequences of her own ignorance.

But, of course, the most disturbing age of any Heyer heroine is that of Juana María de los

Dolores de León, just 14 when she marries the 24-year-old Harry Smith in *The Spanish Bride*. Yes, this is based on a true story and no, I don't think the historical record should be altered to reflect current standards, but romanticizing a child bride situation, and turning Harry into a hero because he saved her from the consequences of the war he was complicit in fighting (and because she's well-bred) has always seemed to me pretty exploitative, if not silently condoning underage marriage.

It's true that the young women of history were (and, sadly, some of today still are) sold into marriage by their families at very young ages, and especially amongst the gentry and nobility, love was considered to be a luxury rather than a necessity in any marital union. Building family ties and gaining wealth and prestige was the point, and the daughters of the house were just bargaining chips used to seek the best deal. Georgette Heyer was doing no more than reflecting the prevailing trends of the eras in which she wrote when she gave us Horry and Pen and Hero (and, absolutely, Juana). I just think it's interesting to note that those very young, by today's standards underage, heroines and their much older husbands would be beyond scandalous today, and the age of consent would be very much invoked when these men were tried as sexual predators.

At least Edward waited until Bella was 18.

– Clara Shipman, Guest Contributor

#12 – GEORGE HEYER: POET AND PLAYWRIGHT BY JENNIFER KLOESTER

Friday, September 18, 2020

Georgette Heyer's father George had several poems published in both *The Granta* and *The Pheon* throughout the 1890s, all of which reflected his whimsical sense of humour and keen observer's eye. A consistent diet of great writers, including Shakespeare, Dickens, Austen, Thackeray, Defoe and the Classical Greeks, meant that George understood and appreciated the ways in which these literary giants revealed the complexities and subtleties of human nature through satire, drama and brilliant comedy. His own writings show him to have been fascinated by character and personality as well as by the comic eccentricities of his fellow human beings. He had an eye for a likely subject and an ear for everyday speech which he was adept at converting into witty dialogue.

From boyhood, George honed his skills writing poetry and short stories; skills which when he became a teacher he sought to impart to his students. George left Cambridge after completing his degree in 1892 and set about finding employment. Although his parents had hoped that he would leave the university to take up the leisured life of an English gentleman with the time and means to concentrate on his writing, a decline in his family's finances forced him into full-time work. He neither resented nor resisted this necessity and on being offered a teaching position at Weymouth College in Dorset accepted the job with alacrity. He was twenty-three years old, healthy, handsome and full of energy and he was soon to discover that he had a knack for teaching, a gift which he was to put to good use in his own family in years to come.

George's greatest achievement while at Weymouth was to be his instigation of a series of Greek plays which were to become a dramatic tradition at the school. The first production was a series of excerpts from Aristophanes' play, *The Clouds*, "with topical additions by G. Heyer". First presented in November 1893 by staff and students, with George in the lead role of Stepsiades, the play was performed entirely in Classical Greek. An explanation of the story was offered in the program, although later it was reported that "the general excellence of the acting made reference to the explanation unnecessary even for those who could not follow the fluent

Greek".

The success of *The Clouds* led George to aim higher still and the following year saw his adaptation of Aristophanes' *The Frogs* receive wide acclaim from a 'large and appreciative audience'. Over the next three years George led his dramatic ensemble through productions of Aristophanes' *The Birds*, *Acharnians* and, in his final year at Weymouth, a full production of *The Clouds*. His abilities as a producer led the Headmaster to acknowledge his 'histrionic talent' and 'genius' for bringing out the best in the boys, but George also won an appreciative response for his own performances in each of the plays.

Throughout his life he reveled in the opportunity to write and perform as he continued to find an outlet for his own literary ambitions in poetry and playwriting. George left Weymouth in April 1898 and his departure was greatly regretted by boys and staff alike. The school magazine, *The Clavinian,* recorded the general feeling in a long paragraph:

> The second loss was that of Mr G. Heyer, who left us at Easter to take up work at his own old school – King's College School, London. He joined us in 1893, and left behind a name which will not easily be forgotten. With his constant good nature and ready wit – he had a jest for everything and an absurd nickname for everybody – he had thrown himself with an almost boyish enthusiasm into all departments of School life. But it is for his part in the great series of Greek plays that he will above all be held in memory. Westminster has had its Latin play for centuries and Bradfield its Greek tragedies, but probably no other school ever produced the comedies of Aristophanes, one after another; and to this the dramatic gifts of George Heyer and his genius as a producer were the most conspicuous contribution. Mr Thorne with the music, Mrs Carré and others making costumes, Messrs Falkner and Davis spending hours in the Gymnasium, painting scenery – all did their part; but without the inspiration of Mr Heyer and his coaching of the actors, the plays would never have been possible. And it all came from that first venture, *The Gipsy's Bride!*'*

Over the next several weeks the *Weekly Post* will be celebrating the poetry of George Heyer, as we continue to try to understand his daughter's genius as well as appreciate these long-lost works in their own right.

– *Jennifer Kloester, Patroness, the International Heyer Society*

* The title of this production is variously referred to as *The Gipsy Queen* and *The Gipsy's Bride* and further research indicates that they were one and the same operetta and that the confusion rests with the writer of *The History of Weymouth College.*

#13 – "THE ROMANCE OF A CARPET BEATING" BY GEORGE HEYER

Friday, September 25, 2020

As discussed in *Nonpareil #3*, and in last week's *Weekly Post*, Georgette Heyer's beloved father George was an accomplished writer in his own right. This is a poem from 1896, published when he was in his mid-twenties:

THE ROMANCE OF A CARPET BEATING

I strolled through a part of the town
  Where the prospect on all sides is dreary,
Where the children's complexions are brown,
  And the children's progenitors beery.

And I came to an open space;–
  There was grass, whereon oil-cans lay scattered,
There were fowls–an emaciate race–
  And a hat that was brimless and battered

Some half dozen urchins in all
  Were playing a quarrelsome cricket
With an empty tobacco-tin ball,
  And marmalade pots for a wicket.

Would one think in this dismal spot
  That a poet would find inspiration?
Well, I may be a poet or not,
  But I found it in my estimation.

For not far from the place where I stood
  A threadbare old carpet was hanging,
Which a man with a cudgel of wood
  Was with ease and persistency banging.

Neither young nor respectably clad,
  Nor in fact altogether unsullied
By his strange occupation, he had
  An air of intentness, though dull-eyed.

And as he with his implement raised
  Selected a spot to apply it,
I stood for some minutes and gazed
  With a desperate longing to try it.
If the mind of the beater was fraught
  With a moderate sense of romance, he
Had the finest occasion, I thought,
  To give a free rein to his fancy.

Were but I in his place, I'd recall
  All the battles historians relate us,–
The carpet should stand for the Gaul,
  Myself should be Roman Torquatus.

I'd be Ajax destroying the sheep
  With many a Greek malediction,

D'Artagnan with foes seven deep,
  And in fact all the heroes of fiction.

And the man, as I looked at him now,
  Seemed so sullen and grim, I'd a notion
That his beetled and lowering brow
  Indicated some hidden emotion.

Was he struggling in thought with a foe,
  Or revenging a fancied aggression?–
I approached him determined to know
  The cause of his sullen expression.

"O man," I exclaimed, "what a life
  Is yours, how replete with illusions,
With what fanciful images rife,
  How prone to poetic effusions!

I have watched your preoccupied mien,
  Till your resolute features impel me
To enquire what your thoughts can have been,–
  If you see no objection to tell me."

As he tendered the carpet a swipe
  He replied, "You're a queer sort o' joker,
I was thinkin' about my old pipe,
  And as 'ow, if I'd baccy, I'd smoke 'er."

I know why I quickly recoiled,
  Why he sniggered as I was departing,
I know that my garments were soiled
  With his dust, and my eyelids were smarting.

But I know not whyever I gave
  The many pence in a moment of madness,
Nor why the mere thought of the knave
  Should inspire me with feelings of sadness.

        B.I.N.K.
    (*The Pheon* March 1896)

#14 – "VISIONS" BY GEORGE HEYER

Friday, October 2, 2020

Following on from "The Romance of a Carpet Beating," here we present the evocative, amusing "Visions," from the long-forgotten poetical works of George Heyer, as unearthed by our Jennifer Kloester:

VISIONS

Tinker, Tailor, Soldier, Sailor, Gentleman, Apothecary, Ploughboy, Thief?

How rarely do our lives agree
With what in early childhood we
Expected some fine day to be!

Each new-born summer we aspire
To be some newer thing, and tire
Of summer-twelve-month's pet desire.

To me, an imitative boy,
It seemed a never-ending joy
To holla hoarsely "dust-ahoy!"

But soon, within a month or so,
A milkman's life was all the go;
I called, like Trilby, "Milk below!"

I went to school: the time was near
For milk-dispensing to appear
An undesirable career.

It saw new crafts; it was not strange
My aspirations suffered change,
Assuming now a wider range.

I longed to be an engine man,
To stand upon the engine's van,
And probe it with an oily can;

To hang upon its throbbing side
At terminuses and deride
Admiring schoolboys in my pride;

Nor yet disdainfully refuse
A *Standard* or a *Daily News*
From wealthy folk who but peruse

The leading articles, and then
Bestow them on the engine men
To barter back to Smith's again.

O engine man, untrammelled, free
Your fingers were allowed to be
Dirty, yet unrebuked. Ah me!

And now, ah, now, O fickle mind,
Nor joy nor beauty can I find
In all the engine-driving kind.

The oily can, the murky hand,
The dole of daily papers, and
The privilege I thought so grand;

I found their charms illusive when
I grew to learn that engine men
Have other duties now and then.

The bobby at the Lord Mayor's show,
Who, standing in the foremost row,
Barges the people to and fro!

The band-conductor at his play,
Who from his coign of vantage may
See a performance every day;

The channel-steamboat man, who tries
To make intelligent replies
To questions of the would-be wise;

"How many passengers the ship
may carry? what her quickest trip
across? and would he mind a tip?"

These and their like, I now recall,
I emulated one and all,
Till each in turn began to pall.

And now I should not care to see
The same play every night, nor be
A Metropolitan P.C.

I even doubt if I should deign
To answer passengers' inane
Enquiries for the sake of gain:

Or dress in the peculiar
Blue jersey of the common tar
With label L.C. and D.R.

No more for such delights I pine,
A Minor Poet now's my line,
On rough-edged paper, superfine,

And two-thirds margin. Only wait;
Who knows but at some future date
I may be Poet Laureate?

(*The Granta* 15 October 1898)

#15 – TWO SHORT POEMS BY GEORGE HEYER

Friday, October 9, 2020

Now, the final instalment in our 4-week celebration of George Heyer's poetry, as we present two short, amusing works, again unearthed by our Jennifer Kloester:

The Song of the Hay-Feverish Songster

The pretty flowers adorn the lea.
  The sweet brier and the rose,
The lilac and the hawthorn tree,
The blue-bell and the sweet, sweet pea,
  A gentle west wind blows.

The gentle west wind comes to me
  Athwart the flowery mean,
It lifts the heavy bumble bee
A-burr from bloom to bloom till he
  Lies swooning in his greed.

The gentle west wind breathes to me
  Of sweet brier and of rose,
Of all the flowers upon the lea,
The blue-bell and the sweet, sweet pea
  Of every bloom that blows.

O gentle west wind, woe is me!
  Mine is a sad, sad plight,
I cannot like that bumble bee
Stoop to the flower cup as did he
  And drink in mad delight.

Kind gentle west wind go from me
  Back to the red, red rose;
Back to the flowers upon the lea,
The lilac and the hawthorn tree;
Lift yet again the bumble bee
To burr, but leave, ah! Leave me free
  From an aching, aching nose!

B.I.N.K. (*The Pheon* June 1896)

A Villanelle of Cricket

'Suave mari magno turbantibus aequora ventis
E terra magnum alterius spectare laborem.'
                                Lucretius II. 1,2.

On summer days I ask no more
Than this, – while burns a sultry sun,
To sit within the tent and score.

To see a batsman drive for four
And extra-cover make it one,–
On summer days I ask no more.

"Suave mari magno…," – when o'er
A parched-up ground men toil, 'tis fun
To sit within the tent and score.

So for an hour, while others bore
The bowling's brunt, I notched each run;–
On summer days I ask no more.

But soon, when I would fain explore
Without, I could prevail on none
To sit within the tent and score.

Then came the bowlers hot and sore
And found <u>analyses</u> not done!

     *   *   *

On summer days I ask no more
To sit within the tent and score.

We hope you have enjoyed this look at Georgette Heyer's most influential literary – and also, literal – progenitor: her father.

– The Patronesses, International Heyer Society

#16 – JACKO BY RACHEL GRANT

Friday, October 16, 2020

> *… no sooner had this magnificent fact dawned on the schoolroom party than they brushed past their scandalized preceptress, tore open the garden-gate, and tumbled out into the road shouting: "A monkey! She has brought a monkey!"*

The impressive arrival of Miss Sophia Stanton-Lacy at my Lord Ombersley's London house in *The Grand Sophy* is made even more splendid by her entourage of animals. There is Salamanca, the Mameluke-trained Spanish horse, Tina the Italian Greyhound, a foul-mouthed parrot and

Jacko, the monkey in a scarlet coat.

Jacko was purchased in Bristol by Sophy and is described as a gentle creature. He would have been one of thousands of "exotic" animals brought to England at that time – a result of the ever-expanding British Empire. Wild creatures were captured in Africa, Asia and the New World and endured appalling conditions of captivity and high levels of stress on their journey to Bristol and other seaports. Often they were given the completely wrong diet as well. Many perished before the journey was over. However, the trade flourished because these animals were seen as luxury items and could command high prices. Queen Charlotte, wife of George III, kept zebras and elephants and was a frequent patron of the Royal Menagerie. The offspring of the kangaroos she kept were often given out to special friends.

Monkeys were particularly popular. However, they actually make very poor pets as they can be highly destructive, difficult to control and can give a very nasty bite.

> Jacko suddenly erupted into the hall from the nether regions, gibbered at the sight of Tina, and swarmed up the window curtains.
> The dratted monkey, she said, had wantonly destroyed two of the best dishcloths, and had scattered a bowl of raisins.

Luckily, in Lord Ombersley's house there would have been plenty of servants to clean up after Jacko (monkeys are very difficult to toilet-train), groom him and feed him. Unfortunately for Miss Adderbury, Arthur Patterson's excellent work "Notes on Pet Monkeys and How to Manage Them" was not published until 1888 and so was no use to her and her charges in helping to care for Jacko in the schoolroom!

It is difficult to know what type of monkey Jacko was. He may have been a green monkey or vervet from Africa. Perhaps he was a marmoset from South America, or a tamarin or capuchin from the New World.

I am lucky enough to live in the West Indies and see capuchins most days on my walks. They are usually in large family groups, chattering and scolding from the treetops. Although the children in *The Grand Sophy* adored their marvellous pet, it is much more marvellous to see these creatures in the wild, where they belong.

– *Rachel Grant, Animal Correspondent*

#17 – MY TOP TEN HEYER HEROINES BY RACHEL HYLAND

Friday, October 23, 2020

When it comes to creating well-rounded, intriguing and thoroughly relatable women, Georgette Heyer truly set the standard in modern fiction. Her heroines are flawed and hardly infallible, and despite some occasional surface similarities, they all have very distinct personalities. What is very curious is that, despite their often-rarefied social status and the strictures of the times in which they lived – and, indeed, where invented – they still manage to speak to us so clearly, and win our hearts so utterly.

Here, a somewhat subjective listing of the very best of these most laudable ladies. Agree? Disagree? Feel free to send in your thoughts, or even your own Top 10!

10. Arabella Tallant, *Arabella* (1949)

Whatever else you might think of Arabella's melodramatic claim of great wealth – which basically amounted to fraud – as her adventures commence, you have to admit, the girl has moxie.

Moreover, she is a social crusader of no little passion, and for all her folly, is truly a good person who wants so much to do what is right that it sometimes leads her astray. Because she's a helper!

9. Ancilla Trent, *The Nonesuch* (1962)

Learned, gracious and independent, the esteemed Miss Trent's ability to deal equably with even the most outlandish behaviour of her charge, the spoiled Tiffany, is little short of miraculous. Determined not to act above her station, Ancilla proves herself to be equal to any—and the fact that she works as a governess not because she has to but because she refuses to be a burden on her family marks her as a woman of great principle, not to mention one quite ahead of her time.

8. Doña Dominica de Rada y Sylva, *Beauvallet* (1929)

Fiery, patriotic and not easily impressed, Doña Dominica remains uncowed when her ship is boarded by pirates, enemies of her nation. True, she begins her tale in fairly cliché female captive fashion – slapping faces and pouting and using tears as a weapon – but when she is tested, she reveals unexpected depths of courage and dignity.

7. Lady Hester Theale, *Sprig Muslin* (1956)

Deceptively meek, with a gentle wit and a good nature second to none, Hester Theale is the kind of woman who refuses to compromise on what is important to her. Nearing thirty and at the beck and call of a rather troublesome family, she nevertheless will not even contemplate a marriage of convenience, or even of mutual friendship, because that is simply not enough for her.

6. Sophia "Sophy" Stanton-Lacy, *The Grand Sophy* (1950)

Sophy is the wish-fulfilling role model for anyone who has ever felt the need to just *fix* everything. True, her manipulations are not to everyone's taste, but the magnificent manner in which she marshals her forces and resolves matters most satisfactorily (for her, anyway) must, at the very least, be admired. Her unconventionality is also to be commended – after all, some of those rules of Society, especially the ones aimed at oppressing women, were just *silly*. And her charisma, at least, cannot be denied.

5. Lady Margaret de Belrémy, *Simon the Coldheart* (1925)

Leader of her own army, rightly resentful of the lord who has laid siege to her castle, and valiant defender of France, Lady Margaret is the only woman to work her way into the legendary Simon the Coldheart's no-longer-so-cold heart. Grim and distant but with an edge that can cut like a knife, clever and cunning and not always honourable, she is a force to be reckoned with—but capable of great compassion and a surprising amount of humility, as well.

4. Sarah Thane, *The Talisman Ring* (1936)

Perpetually amused and taking even the most shocking events entirely in her stride, the redoubtable Sarah Thane is exactly the kind of person you would want to have by your side in a crisis – or at any time at all. With quick thinking, a calm manner and a twinkle in her eyes, she is not only a literal lifesaver, but a most excellent friend and companion with whom to while away a day, a week, or even a lifetime.

3. Venetia Lanyon, *Venetia* (1958)

Unselfish, unspoiled, unsullied and unprejudiced, Venetia refuses to allow anyone to dictate to her how she should live her life, or whom she should love. Intelligent, practical, witty and endearing, she is not only a forgiving soul on an almost cosmic scale, but she is also secretly ruthless when it comes to getting her own way.

2. Frederica Merriville, *Frederica* (1965)

With grace, charm and no little resolve, Frederica accomplishes even the most daunting of tasks with hardly ever a complaint. Whether it is caring for her siblings, each presenting her with a special challenge, or finagling their entrée into a social world that had previously been happy to ignore their existence, she wins most everyone to her side by just being herself: charming, frank, engaging and just a really fun person to know.

1. Prudence Tremaine, *The Masqueraders* (1928)

Here is a woman forced to disguise herself as a man, and carry herself as one too, in order to keep her brother safe from prosecution after a treasonous uprising. Here is a woman of wit, ingenuity and acumen, skilful with a sword and with a dice box, wholly at home in the company of men at a time when that was a feat considered nigh on impossible. The fact that Prue even manages to finds true love while in disguise – with a man eventually perspicacious enough to see through the façade to the woman beneath – is a testament to her many talents.*

– Rachel Hyland, Patroness, the International Heyer Society

* (Excerpt taken from *Heyer Society – Essays on the Literary Genius of Georgette Heyer*)

#18 – MY TOP TEN HEYER HEROES BY RACHEL HYLAND

Friday, October 30, 2020

Last week, I looked at Georgette Heyer's ten best heroines. This time out, it is their beloveds we discuss, in their multifaceted manliness and various degrees of wit, intellect, thoughtfulness and need for redemption. Across her fifty-plus novels, Georgette Heyer gifted us with a panoply of heroes who grow and learn and laugh throughout their (mostly accidental) courtships. Here, I list those I think are her best.

Agree? Disagree? Get in touch with your thoughts, or even your own list.

10. Mr. Robert Beaumaris, *Arabella* (1949)

It would have been easy for Mr. Beaumaris to ruin the upstart chit who had dared lie to him, make him a gift of more than one inconvenient charge, and force him to look good and hard at his failings. That he is far too decent to do it, and that he can see beyond Arabella's apparent fraud and discern that he was himself to blame for it is a testament not only to his self-awareness, but to his burgeoning fondness for the young lady who so thoroughly turns his life upside down, entirely against his will.

9. Sir Waldo Hawkridge, *The Nonesuch* (1962)

A noted sportsman and acknowledged leader of fashion, Sir Waldo is a man who can look as high as he wishes for a bride. But when he meets the reserved but delightful Ancilla Trent, a country governess in a country town many of his ilk would despise, he is immediately won over by her many sterling qualities. Charming, gracious and able to find amusement in even the direst of entertainments, he is a true gentleman, in every sense of the word. And, let us not forget, he's a secret philanthropist! There aren't very many of those in Heyer (that we know of; that's what the word "secret" means, after all), so he is doubly to be admired for his many good deeds.

8. Sir Anthony Fanshawe, *The Masqueraders* (1928)

With a quickness of will and wit belied by his sleepy demeanour and powerful bulk, Sir Anthony is not only one of the few to see through the clever disguises donned by the Merriott siblings, but he is also fast to react when they need saving from the elaborate plotting that is sure to bring them down. Astute, kind, honourable and upstanding, Sir Anthony is the rock on which his lady love can, at last, lean.

5. Jasper, Lord Damerel, *Venetia* (1958)

A dissolute rake resigned to his fate as an outcast and renegade, the usually careless Lord Damerel is won over by the frankness, the wit and the undeniable beauty of his neighbour, the fearless Venetia Lanyon. First becoming friends, soon their attraction will not be denied, but Damerel is determined to save Venetia from the ruin that can only be her reward for associating with him – even at the expense of his own happiness. This one is a redemption tale for the ages, and Damerel's scholarship and winning ways only add to his appeal.

6. Sir Tristram Shield, *The Talisman Ring* (1936)

There aren't many men who can deal as ably with as much crime as Sir Tristram must deal with across the course of a few short weeks. Between the murder and the burglary and the smuggling and the abetting of wanted criminals, it is enough to send anyone crazy. But not Sir Tristram! With his good humour, his commanding manner, his clever wit and his quick appreciation of the spirited Sarah Thane, he wins our hearts – and defeats the bad guy – with total aplomb, while also somehow managing to keep his melodramatic cousins Ludovic and Eugenie at least somewhat in line. No mean feat!

5. Major Hugo Darracott, *The Unknown Ajax* (1925)

Who among us cannot relate to the intelligent, capable Hugo? To be prejudged and found wanting by his family, into which he comes falsely labelled as something of a usurper, is infuriating in the extreme, and the manner in which he serves them a just comeuppance by playing the fool and the bumpkin, just as they expected, is a joy to behold. Especially as his lovely cousin Anthea begins to suspect there is far more to this new connexion than anyone gave him credit for...

4. Justin Alistair, Duke of Avon, *These Old Shades* (1926)

Deceptively languid and frivolous, but with a core of pure steel, the Duke of Avon is a practiced flirt and gamester and (it must be said) attempted abductor of women – let us not forget dear Jenny – who is redeemed through the simple devotion of a cross-dressing teenager with whom he intends to get revenge on an old enemy. Why, then, is Avon such a favourite? Much of it is, of course, that he is saved by the love of a good woman, and we all love that narrative. But more than that, it is his singular, much-vaunted omniscience, his uncanny intellect, that makes Avon so utterly compelling.

3. Vernon Dauntry, Marquis of Alverstoke, *Frederica* (1965)

When first confronted by his importunate distant cousin, Frederica Merriville, for help launching her exquisite sister Charis into the ton, Alverstoke is just going through the motions of his privileged life. He is bored with the social whirl, tired of being expected to bankroll his assorted relations, and is without direction or purpose. Slowly, as he comes to care for this most unusual woman (and her younger brothers), Alverstoke discovers that there can be more to life than firing off witty barbs at those who displease him—though it is to be hoped he is never quite cured of that habit. With humour, resourcefulness and a tender care, Alverstoke proves himself to be the equal of any challenge: especially the challenge of making Frederica aware of his feelings for her. Eventually.

2. Simon of Beauvallet, *Simon the Coldheart* (1925)

Simon (later Sir/Lord Simon) is a self-made man, an unparalleled soldier with an iron will who is immune to the charms of fluttering court ladies, but falls for the spirited Lady Margaret of Belrémy, who valiantly protects her home, and her heart, from this encroaching English lord. Simon is just so *great*, and a distinct favourite, due to his code of honour, his martial prowess and his aptitude for a total home makeover, which is possibly the best part of his book.

1. Freddy Standen, *Cotillion* (1928)

Freddy is barely even his own hero at the start of the novel, but by the end he has become everything we could want in a man—the kind of man he would never have had the hubris to believe he could be. When our action commences, the kindly Freddy just wants to (and/or, is persuaded to) do a good turn for his sweet, neglected almost-cousin, for whom he has always had a fondness. Kitty's plight sees him forced to draw on hidden depths to solve crises of varying degrees, all while being pleasant and decent and just a lovely, if occasionally frustrated by museums, human being. Freddy proves that it doesn't have to be all alpha males and love/hate witty barbs, it doesn't have to be esoteric quotes and sporting prowess and a thunderous brow. Sometimes, the swoonworthiest hero is the one who is just… really nice.

SPECIAL MENTIONS must go to Freddy's scene-stealing father, Lord Legerwood, and to the excellent Mr. Charles Trevor, private secretary to Lord Alverstoke of *Frederica*, both heroes in their own right.

– *Rachel Hyland, Patroness, the International Heyer Society*

* (Excerpt taken from *Heyer Society – Essays on the Literary Genius of Georgette Heyer*)

~ | ~

#19 – YOUR TOP TEN HEYER HEROINES AND HEROES

Friday, November 6, 2020

Over the past two weeks we have delivered Society patroness Rachel Hyland's Top 10 Heyer Heroines and Heroes.

Here, a selected listing of your responses to same:

RACHEL'S TOP 10 HEYER HEROINES
10. Arabella Tallant, *Arabella* (1949)
9. Ancilla Trent, *The Nonesuch* (1962)
8. Doña Dominica de Rada y Sylva, *Beauvallet* (1929)
7. Lady Hester Theale, *Sprig Muslin* (1956)
6. Sophia "Sophy" Stanton-Lacy, *The Grand Sophy* (1950)
5. Lady Margaret de Belrémy, *Simon the Coldheart* (1925)
4. Sarah Thane, *The Talisman Ring* (1936)
3. Venetia Lanyon, *Venetia* (1958)
2. Frederica Merriville, *Frederica* (1965)
1. Prudence Tremaine, *The Masqueraders* (1928)

YOUR TOP HEROINES:

Frances Turner: Jenny Chawleigh: practical, hard-working, deals with real life as she sees it, recognizes idiots for what they are and deals with them appropriately, clear-sighted and honest with herself, vulnerable and brave. She gets her well-deserved reward.

Heather Wallace: Sarah Thane is my all-time favourite and someone I would love to spend time with. Of your list I would like to be friends with she, Frederica, Sophy and Ancilla. Others I would like to meet in person are:

Abigail Wendover
Phoebe Marlow (she's an author and observer)
Mary Challoner
Cressida Stavely
Annis Wychwood
Kitty Charing
Hero Wantage

I enjoy imagining how Heyer's heroines would interact, I think Hero and Kitty would become close friends. Phoebe would get on well with them both too, while of the more mature heroines Annis and Abigail would be friends.

Maura Tan: Love this, Rach, but have to say that I think Dominica (whiny, histrionic Dominica) should be replaced with Deb Grantham, who is actively employed and fierce in her independence and who has a moral compass that will not allow her to take the easy path to security by taking advantage of a youngster's infatuation. Deb Grantham for #1 Heyer Heroine, I say! Dominica does not hold a candle to her. Surely you can see that?

Kirsten Davis: Love this list! However, I think you're missing one key person: Mary Challoner. She shoots her future husband, nurses him back to health, runs off with another man, and then breaks up a duel being fought over her. She's simply amazing!

Colleen Reed: A great list but I am sad not to see Phoebe Marlow's name anywhere. She should be top of the list! A writer, an individualist, a survivor of abuse who escapes persecution to forge a better life for herself – she is a treasure, and the fact that she tames and even humbles the insufferable Duke of Salford and makes him into a semblance of a human is greatly to her credit. Disappointed to see her so shunned in such excellent company as Frederica and Venetia, where surely she belongs.

Ruth Williamson: *The Reluctant Widow's* **Elinor Rochdale** has seen more of the world than another personal favorite, Jane Austen's Elinor Dashwood. Both heroines are level-headed women of sense, who face up to the consequences of family financial losses. For Heyer's Elinor, there is the added sting of having been jilted. She has become a governess to support herself and arrives at dilapidated Highnoons in Sussex to take up a new position. It is not the highly unusual one offered by Edward, Lord Carlyon, the autocratic peer she meets there, who is definitely not Austen's diffident Edward Ferrars. Elinor Rochdale has an independent turn of mind. This gives rise to spirited discussions with his lordship. Overnight she becomes a widow and the chatelaine of Highnoons, where she encounters (amongst others) an impetuous adolescent, a series of highly suspect "visitors," and a raw-boned canine. Soon she transforms Lord Carlyon's original idea of her potential. Free-spirited Elinor enjoys provoking him by challenging any and all of his advice. Furthermore, she acts courageously and proves to be a capital whip. In her vivacity she differs from Austen's Elinor. The reluctant widow is not only resourceful and quick-witted, she is lively. This makes her irresistible, and my favorite among Heyer's heroines.*

Jennifer Kloester, Patroness: It's not easy choosing a favorite heroine from one of Georgette Heyer's many novels – there are so many obvious candidates: Sophy, Léonie, Venetia, Frederica, Arabella, Mary Challoner, Sarah Thane, Drusilla Morville, Anthea Darracott – all of them deserve their popularity, but my choice is for a heroine often overlooked, both by her readers and by her fictional friends and family. She is a woman constrained by the rules and etiquette of her time, a woman forced to stifle her intellect and to hide it behind a camouflage of docility. Yet she is smart and funny and, despite the dismal reality of her situation in life, she is a woman who maintains her integrity with a ferocity belied by her shyness and soft-speaking. Those around her are mostly blind to the real woman and recognize neither her sense of humor nor her capacity for love. Kind, honorable and perceptive, **Hester Theale** from *Sprig Muslin* is one of Heyer's finest characters – a woman of immense courage and unexpected spirit. Complex and surprising, she is fully realized in the novel as a three-dimensional character with a depth of feeling that continues to surprise readers. Hester has never failed to intrigue me and the scene where she hides behind the curtain in Sir Gareth's bedchamber is one of Heyer's funniest. Hester is the sister I always wished I'd had.*

RACHEL'S TOP 10 HEYER HEROES

10. Mr. Robert Beaumaris, *Arabella* (1949)
9. Sir Waldo Hawkridge, *The Nonesuch* (1962)
8. Sir Anthony Fanshawe, *The Masqueraders* (1928)
7. Jasper, Lord Damerel, *Venetia* (1958)
6. Sir Tristram Shield, *The Talisman Ring* (1936)

5. Major Hugo Darracott, *The Unknown Ajax* (1925)
4. Justin Alistair, Duke of Avon, *These Old Shades* (1926)
3. Vernon Dauntry, Marquis of Alverstoke, *Frederica* (1965)
2. Simon of Beauvallet, *Simon the Coldheart* (1925)
1. Freddy Standen, *Cotillion* (1928)

YOUR TOP HEROES

Sally Dale: Agree totally on your review of Freddy Standen & his father too. One of my favourites books and characters. I still laugh out loud over his views on the British Museum, Elgin Marbles et al.

Heather Wallace: I'm so glad Freddy is No1, he is my favourite hero, so kind and someone to go shopping with...my perfect man. I think Jack Farthing would play him admirably.

Clara Shipman: Hard to argue with most of this list, but I do wonder: where is my Gilly? True, he might not be the most storybook of heroes, but he is valiant and brave (in his quiet fashion) and the hero of a very unusual book, as well. He's just adorable! Not my favourite, but he's surely worthy of a Top 10 berth. What gives?

Maura Tan: Again I must object! Is Sir Richard Wyndham honestly not on your Top 10 list? His poise, his sense of duty, his quickness of wit and his reluctant love that he cannot deny… how is he not here? Is it the age gap? No, surely it can't be, since you have Damerel and Avon on here. What do you possibly not like about Sir Richard? WHAT? I need to know.

[Rachel responds: I like him fine. There are just so many wonderful Heyer heroes that narrowing them down to ten absolute favourites is tricky. That said, I would take any of the ten heroes on my list over Sir Richard Wyndham any day of the week. He's great, but he's not GREAT. You know? But I acknowledge your right to an opinion, of course.]

Colleen Reed: MAX RAVENSCAR!!! How could you neglect him? HOW?!!

Ruth Williamson: *Black Sheep*'s eponymous black sheep, **Miles Calverleigh**, views Bath society and its hangers-on through heavy-lidded, cynical eyes. He sees the world from the perspective of experience of the school of life. From the moment this sallow-skinned, carelessly dressed and unconventional character appears on the page, he challenges assumptions about what underpins genteel behavior. His warm smile and sense of the ridiculous mitigate his eye to the main chance. He is a mature hero, unfashionable, and as much of a dark horse as he is a prodigal son. His exchanges with the heroine, Abby Wendover, are punctuated by wit, humor and fellow feeling. In fact, when he is absent from any scene, it is the poorer for lacking his undeniable charm. For all that, he has his faults. A distinct lack of polished drawing room manners marks his sharp contrast with a Heyer hero like Mr. Robert Beaumaris. Yet Miles Calverleigh overstates the case when he tells Abby that he has no virtues: he proves fully capable of rescuing his chosen lady from her particular silken cage. His strategy is masterly, in keeping with his business acumen. His wife will be a very fortunate lady.*

Jennifer Kloester, Patroness: The choice of a favorite Heyer hero depends on the criteria. Does one want a romantic hero like Sir Anthony Fanshawe or Gervase Frant? Or a cynical, sardonic hero like the Duke of Avon or Miles Calverleigh? Perhaps an omniscient hero like Mr. Beaumaris or a dashing one like Beau Wyndham or a charming scapegrace like Anthony Sheringham? One of

Heyer's great talents was her ability to create character and, while she sometimes referred to her "Mark I" or "Mark II" heroes, the truth is that her male leads are a diverse lot with no two being exactly alike. Each of her heroes is perfectly suited to his story and several times she made the hero the main focus of her novel (*Sylvester, The Unknown Ajax, False Colours, Charity Girl*).

For her readers, Heyer's heroes are living, breathing men who are attractive in very different ways. Though I love them, popular favorites such as Jasper Damerel and Dominic Alastair would not be my choice given that my personal preference is for kinder, more reliable men. Sir Tristram Shield for example, or that gentle giant, Hugo Darracott, or kind Freddy Standen. They are intelligent, modest men and they each have a sense of humor. I love Tristram for his integrity and strength of character, Hugo for his love of a joke, his quick-thinking and perception, and Freddy for his innate goodness, his retiring disposition and his hidden depths. To choose among these three is difficult but in the end I cannot go past **Hugo Darracott** of *The Unknown Ajax*, who as well as being amiable, charming and handsome also has at least half a million pounds to his name!*

*Excerpts taken from *Heyer Society – Essays on the Literary Genius of Georgette Heyer*

#20 – SUCH AN AMUSING VILLAIN – HEYER'S BAD GUYS BY CLARA SHIPMAN

Friday, November 13, 2020

In her book *Heyer for Beginners*, Maura Tan documents reading Georgette Heyer's historical works for the first time – historically (ha! a pun!) not her bag. She had read and enjoyed Heyer's contemporaries and mysteries, but she had objected to historical fiction as a genre since she read Philippa Gregory's slander of various dead royals, and, yeah, I get it.

But bravely, wisely, *finally*, she gave into the peer pressure of her fellow *Heyer Society* essayists, as well as the lure of Heyer's perfection, and she kicked off with the first of Heyer's novels, *The Black Moth*. In her entry on the book, she says of Tracy Belmanoir, Duke of Andover, that he is not only the villain of the book, but a "... REAL villain. If #metoo was a thing back then, women all over the country would have been #metoo-ing about the Duke of Andover constantly, given how much he apparently liked to kidnap and rape them." She's not wrong. But it got me to thinking... is there a worse villain in Heyer than Devil Belmanoir? Is it just me, or do most of her books not even *have* villains? Not of that caliber, anyway.

In *These Old Shades,* the Comte de St. Vire is pretty villainous, dooming his own child to a life of hardship and penury in order to get revenge on his brother because of the Bible, according to the Duke of Avon. And both *The Reluctant Widow* and *The Talisman Ring* have awful family members up to no good, spying and murdering and that sort of thing, while also being vain and condescending, which is almost as bad. And there are nasty guardians, like Uncle Matthew from *Cotillion* and those Bagshots from *Friday's Child* and Phoebe's abusive stepmother in *Sylvester*. I guess most of *The Unknown Ajax*'s Darracotts are pretty unpleasant, too, and no one likes Torquil from *Cousin Kate*—though it's unkind to call him a villain when he was clearly undiagnosed bi-polar and he's as much a victim as anyone else, those times being not very enlightened about mental illness.

But think about it, who is the villain in, say, *The Grand Sophy*? Is it Miss Wraxton? That's a bit harsh. (Of course, some people would say it was Sophy, but they are wrong. Very, very wrong.) Who's the villain in *Frederica*? Lady Buxted? Sure, neither are very nice, but they don't plot or scheme destruction, or cause any real harm. They're just kind of jerks about our heroines, which doesn't exactly send them into villain territory.

What about in *Lady of Quality*? In *Bath Tangle*? In *Sprig Muslin*? Is family and societal expectation a villain? Because that's the only real problem for anyone there. Indeed, I think that most of the time, the villain in Heyer's historical novels – and especially in her Regency novels – is Society itself. The major conflicts that usually arise are all about what is expected of everyone by everyone else. Without Society's rules, Venetia and Damerel could have fallen in love and gotten married in a heartbeat, and who cares about his reputation? Almost all of Phoebe's troubles in *Sylvester* would have been averted if she'd been able to pick her own husband and also be an author if she wished. (A general frowning upon child abuse would also have been helpful, there.) And in *The Nonesuch*, if it weren't for what she thought was a big difference in their stations, Ancilla and Sir Waldo would have been calling out the Banns in a couple of days, because they're just so perfect for each other.

The more I think about it, the more impressed I am with Heyer's ability to create so many stories in which almost all the conflict comes, not from the words, deeds or designs of a Bad Guy, but from the fact that the world our characters live in is really controlling and judgmental and just *mean* to them.

So there you have it, Society at large is the ultimate villain in the works of Georgette Heyer. Except sometimes the villain is Napoleon. So maybe it's a tie.

– *Clara Shipman, Guest Contributor*

#21 – WHY CLORINDA? BY SUSANNAH FULLERTON

Friday, November 20, 2020

In Chapter III of *Regency Buck* Lord Worth, driving his curricle-and-four towards Grantham, comes across Judith Taverner sitting on a bank at the side of the road, removing her shoe so as to dislodge a stone. He asks Judith her name, and she responds tartly: "Again, sir, that is no concern of yours." Whereupon Lord Worth announces, "I shall have to call you Clorinda", and offers, to her great embarrassment, to put on her shoe for her.

So why 'Clorinda', and what does Lord Worth mean by this choice of name. I have no definite answers, but there are various possibilities.

Clorinda is a fictional character in a work by the Italian poet Tasso, a poem called *Jerusalem Delivered*. This was published in 1581 and over the centuries became a popular subject with artists. Clorinda, the heroine of the poem, is a warrior princess in the Saracen army. The composer Monteverdi turned the poem into an opera in 1624, which also helped to make the heroine's name more familiar to audiences around Europe. Is Lord Worth showing off his own cultural knowledge by choosing such a name, and is the name a reference to Judith's scowling face and combative attitude?

Clorinda is an expansion of the Greek word 'Chloris' meaning 'green'. Perhaps Worth is bestowing such a name upon her because she is sitting on a green bank? Or does he mistakenly take her for a 'green' country girl? The name can also mean 'praise' or 'beauty' in Greek, and Worth has already called Judith 'Beauty in distress', so perhaps the name is a compliment to her looks?

'Clorinda' was the name of a painting by the artist Thomas Douglas Guest (1781 – 1845), exhibited in London in 1811 (which is the year in which *Regency Buck* is set). Guest also painted the portrait of boxer Jem Belcher (who is mentioned as having given Worth lessons) so perhaps Lord Worth went to see the picture of his pugilist teacher and also saw Guest's 'Clorinda' and it is this portrait which he has in mind? (Unfortunately, I cannot find a copy of this picture, so don't know what the Clorinda of the portrait is doing / wearing / representing.)

In the 17th century play by Thomas Killigrew, *Cecilia and Clorinda: or Love in Arms*, Clorinda is an Amazon, or warrior maiden. Worth does later refer to Judith as an Amazon (she is a tall girl and we are told she was "no featherweight"), so perhaps Worth is alluding to her size and her feistiness?

Rossini's opera 'La Cenerentola', based on the story of Cinderella, calls the two ugly stepsisters Clorinda and Tisbe, but that work only premiered in 1817 and surely Georgette would not have made mention of such an opera when she was setting her novel in 1811 – 1812? The idea of a shoe needing to be replaced on a foot does fit the 'Cinderella' theme, but I'd have thought that Georgette would have checked her dates before using such a reference. She was generally meticulous about such things.

But there is another possibility that she did make a mistake. The great Scottish poet, Robert Burns, fell in love with a woman named Agnes Maclehose (1759 – 1841) in 1787. They were instantly attracted, and she invited Burns to come and drink tea with her. However, he suffered a bad injury to his knee before the visit and was unable to walk for some time, so the couple began an amorous correspondence instead. At her suggestion they styled themselves by the Arcadian names of Sylvander and Clarinda. The relationship was never consummated, but it was for his 'Clarinda' that Burns wrote the wonderful and moving song *Ae Fond Kiss*. Georgette Heyer would surely have known of this famous love affair (the letters of the pair had been published and every biography of Burns mentions the romance) and Burns was famed (or notorious) as a lover of women who easily succumbed to his charm). Did Heyer have Worth choose the pastoral name with a Burns association and did she then mis-spell it 'Clorinda' instead of 'Clarinda'? I must admit that, when listening to *Regency Buck* on audio, I just assumed that the reference was to Burns' Clarinda, and it was only when I checked the printed page and realised there was a difference in spelling, that I had to re-think my original assumption.

It is clear that Worth is rather fond of the name he has given to Judith. As he delivers her back to the inn, her brother Perry rushes out and addresses her by name, asking if there has been an accident: "'Judith,' repeated the gentleman of the curricle pensively. 'I prefer Clorinda'." And in the last chapter of the novel, he is still using his preferred name for the woman he has come to love.

I'm afraid I do not have any definite answer to the question 'Why Clorinda?', but I'd love to hear from fellow members of the International Heyer Society if you have alternative theories to add to the mix? And perhaps it is time someone set to work on scholarly, annotated editions of all of Georgette Heyer's novels, with references and notes attached, so that we can look up such questions as these and, hopefully, find answers.

– Susannah Fullerton, Patroness, the International Heyer Society

#22 – LOCATION, LOCATION, LOCATION IN HEYER BY CLARA SHIPMAN

Friday, November 27, 2020

If you've been paying attention to the weekly Heyer Society Polls, you may recall that one from some months back asked us to choose our "Favorite Heyer Novel Location." Simple right? But, no, it ended up being much harder to give an answer to that question than I would have thought possible. At first I figured: *Well London, obviously*. But then as my eye drifted down the list of potentials, I began to see that there was a lot to be said for places other than London in Heyer's works.

The choices given us by the Heyer Society Powers That Be were (and are; voting is still open, forever, I think) London, Bath, a Country Manor, a Country Inn and The Continent, and honestly, I can make a solid argument for all five.

Here goes:

LONDON: It's home to *Frederica* and *The Grand Sophy* and *The Masqueraders* and much of *Arabella* and *Sylvester* and *Cotillion* and *Regency Buck.* So of course, London!

BATH: It's home to *Black Sheep* and *Lady of Quality* and the funniest part of *Friday's Child* and the part where we begin to like Diana in *The Black Moth,* and *Bath Tangle*, obvs. So of course, Bath!

A COUNTRY MANOR: It's (literally) home to *The Unknown Ajax*, *Venetia*, *The Quiet Gentleman* and *The Reluctant Widow.* And let's not forget *False Colours*, the most underestimated Heyer novel of all time. So of course, a Country Manor!

A COUNTRY INN: It's home to *The Talisman Ring, The Corinthian* and *Sprig Muslin,* as well as the bit where Alverstoke realizes just how much he adores Frederica. That last bit is enough to make this locale a fave. So of course, a Country Inn!

THE CONTINENT: Paris sees Avon's deep games in *These Old Shades* and Philip Jettan's terrible poetry in *Powder and Patch.* Elsewhere in France, *Devil's Cub* Vidal plots to rid himself of Mary Challoner and Simon Beauvallet captures and courts the Lady Margaret—while his descendant, the piratical Nick, spends at least as much time in Spain as does Major Harry Smith as he captures *The Spanish Bride.* So of course, the Continent!

Looking at this list, I had to ask myself the question, do I even HAVE a favorite Heyer Novel Location? I'm not sure it is possible to pick. Because yes, of course it is London! But it is also, of course, the other four. (As well as a toll-gate.)

Which is all a very long way of explaining why I didn't vote. But unlike the reasons people often give for not voting in *very important elections what do you mean you didn't vote you live in Florida and that's a swing state people die for the right to vote Grandma!* (sorry, personal stuff there), it was not because the choices were equally bad but because they were, and are, equally good.

And I am totally going to go and read *The Toll-Gate* now. Best. Heyer. Novel. Location. Ever. (Except for all the other ones.)

– Clara Shipman, Guest Contributor

#23 – CHRISTMAS IN HEYER'S REGENCY BY RACHEL HYLAND

Friday, December 4, 2020

With the season fast approaching – the holiday season, that is – I thought it was a good time to look at how Christmas was celebrated in the Heyer's Regency novels.

True, Christmas does not play an especially big part in any of them. Occasionally we will hear about it, usually in passing, but only rarely does it occur while we are witnessing the event.

Despite this, and with Heyer's customary light touch, we are able to divine several details about this most wonderful time of the year...

We know, for example, that there were theatricals, both amateur and professional:

"Never having seen a more exciting theatrical performance than some Scenes from Shakespeare, enacted at Christmas in his godfather's house, he had been carried away by the melodrama, and had turned a deaf ear to his conscience, which had whispered to him that in taking Felix to the Surrey Theatre he had exposed his tender mind to corruption…" – *Frederica*

"Recollect that he said I shouldn't be presented till I was eighteen, or act in the theatricals at Roxwell, at Christmas, or drive his bays, or – oh, a hundred things!" – *April Lady*

"Perhaps you might come to me after Christmas, and see the pantomime, and all the famous sights." – *The Foundling*

And we know that presents were customary:

"Is this the snuff you were given at Christmas? No, I thank you!" – *Regency Buck*

"… it was rarely that his affection led him to do more for them than to give them a guinea apiece every Christmas." – *Arabella*

"So she had swallowed her resentment at the treatment she had received, and had continued, throughout the succeeding years, to send Joseph small Christmas gifts, and periodical letters, affectionately enquiring after the state of his health, and regaling him with accounts of Julian's virtues, beauty and scholastic prowess." – *The Nonesuch*

"She had the happy thought of promising to bestow a timepiece upon him [Jason] as a Christmas gift if he would but refrain, in the interim, from stealing Ferdy's." – *Friday's Child*

We know that family played a big part in the occasion:

"It was the immutable custom of the House of Rayne for as many members of it as could possibly do so to gather at Christmas under the roof of the head of the family. As the family was enormous, and most of those who congregated ad Chance remained for a month, Sylvester had little leisure, and saw less of his mother than he liked." – *Sylvester*

"'Do you mean to spend your Christmas at Claycross?'
'Yes: an unwilling sacrifice on the altar of duty. My sister comes tomorrow, bringing with her I know not how many of her offspring; and my cousin Cordelia, labouring apparently under the mistaken belief that I must be pining for a sight of my wards, brings the whole pack down upon me on Thursday.'" – *Bath Tangle*

And that it was customary for landowners to provide Christmas bounty to their workers:

"When Mr. Chawleigh arrived, laden with gifts ranging from a tie pin blazing with diamonds set round a large emerald, which he bestowed upon his stunned son-in-law, to a pound of tea, he found Jenny immersed in preparations for the Christmas dinner it was the custom of the house to give to the farm workers and their families… He was interested in this particular form of benevolence. He himself (in his own words) always did the handsome thing by his numerous dependents at Christmas; but the country habit of inviting all and sundry to a large party was unknown to him, his gifts taking a monetary form." – *A Civil Contract*

We know that there were Christmas parties:

> "'If I give a dance, I'll hire the musicians from Harrogate, like I did at Christmas,' she declared. 'There's never been anything nip-cheese about my parties, nor will there be!'" – *The Nonesuch*

> "I once held one [a party] over Christmas: that was a triumph indeed!" – *Cousin Kate*

But that those in mourning could not celebrate in any such fashion:

> "From her first flat veto, she passed to the enumeration of all the difficulties in the way of holding a ball at Stanyon at that season of the year… 'Had it been Christmas, it might have been proper for us to do something of that nature,' she said.
> "'Hardly, ma'am!' said Gervase, in a deprecating tone. 'You had not then, I am persuaded, put off your blacks.' This was unanswerable." – *The Quiet Gentleman*

Probably our most comprehensive picture of a Regency Christmas comes from *The Spanish Bride*, in which Juana celebrates her "first English Christmas" while Harry is off fighting in America:

> "Her interest in the Christmas preparations was dutiful, but a little perfunctory, and she did not enjoy the party itself. It was soothing to her present mood to accompany the family to church in the morning, and to pray for Harry's safety (for she had not the smallest hesitation in entering a Protestant Church), but the big dinner party in the evening she found rather overwhelming. There were so many relatives present, all chattering about family affairs, and laughing at old jests, that she felt herself a stranger, and would have slipped away had not John seen the disconsolate look on her face, and moved over to sit beside her, and to talk to her about the subject nearest to both their hearts."

It doesn't sound too different from what is experienced in most families today – whether they celebrate Christmas, or some other family-centric, food-focussed, present-giving occasion – does it? Of course, for many of us, this holiday season will be very different from those we have previously enjoyed, but it is reassuring to know that no matter how much things may feel like they have changed, some traditions can likely withstand anything. As it was, ever will it be; that is the message we can take from even Heyer's most fleeting accounts of Christmases past.

Tidings of comfort and joy, indeed.

– Rachel Hyland, Patroness, the International Heyer Society

#24 – CHRISTMAS PUDDING BY SUSANNAH FULLERTON

Friday, December 11, 2020

When Georgette Heyer sat down on Christmas Day to enjoy a celebratory meal with Ronald and Richard, she no doubt enjoyed a slice of Christmas pudding as part of her seasonal fare. But would the characters in her Georgian and Regency novels have known such a famous dessert? Would Sir Bonamy Ripple's corsets have been strained to their utmost by a very large slice of this solid and filling pudding? Would Lord Alverstoke have expected his chef to produce such food on Christmas Day?

Puddings have long been a part of the Englishman's traditional diet, but they were originally made from meat. The Ancient Romans had eaten puddings boiled in skins or cloth, and brought that practice to Britain. Throughout the Middle Ages people ate a variety of meat puddings that had been boiled. Gradually, somewhere along the way the meat dropped out, the suet stayed in, spices were added, along with dried fruit and sugar, and the plum pudding as we know it today came into existence. The first written recipe dates from 1723 and it appeared in John Nott's *The Cooks and Confectioners Dictionary*. The puddings were a common accompaniment to beef, especially on festive days. They were eaten as part of the main course, not afterwards, and they were not topped with cream, ice-cream or custard, as would be the case today. Plum puddings, throughout the 18th century, took on an aura of 'Britishness'. Gilray features such a pudding in his satirical cartoon, 'The Plum Pudding in Danger' and the nursery rhyme about little Jack Horner (who pulls a plum from his Christmas pie) also dates from the 18th century. Some historians believe that plum puddings developed from pease pudding or plum pottage, but these were much sloppier dishes, more like a porridge, and I don't think ever merged into the same thing. There are also unsubstantiated stories that plum puddings were requested by King George I, who was given the nickname of 'the Pudding King' as a result, but there is no written proof for this tale.

In 1675 a British naval chaplain mentioned in his journal eating "plum puddings" for Christmas dinner on board ship – this is the first reference to the dessert being a part of Christmas fare, but it was still not being called 'Christmas Pudding'. Jane Austen's mother, Cassandra Austen, wrote a poem about a pudding for family friend Martha Lloyd's recipe (or 'receipt') book and her description, including bread, sugar, butter, currants, cloves, mace, rose water, eggs and milk, does sound pretty similar to recipes of the 21st century. By the 1830s puddings were almost exclusively sweet and were associated with the festive season. Cookbook writer Eliza Acton gives it the title of 'Christmas Pudding' in 1845 in her book *Modern Cookery for Private Families*.

By the Victorian era the pudding was well ensconced as traditional Christmas fare and Charles Dickens includes a wonderful pudding "like a speckled cannon ball" as part of the Cratchit family's menu in *A Christmas Carol*. Puddings kept well and so could be offered to surprise visitors who came during the festive season. It was in the 19th century that small coins were added, or sometimes good luck tokens (a custom that has dropped out of use today, after broken teeth or unwanted visits to A & E.).

After one has eaten a heavy Christmas dinner, the nicest activity is to lie on a sofa with a good book and perhaps sleep off the food and champagne. Perhaps this year, after eating your Christmas pudding, you might like to pick up a Georgette Heyer novel as fabulous entertainment, 'loosen your corsets' and reflect that you have enjoyed a meal that would not have been unfamiliar to her or her characters.

– Susannah Fullerton, Patroness, the International Heyer Society

~ | ~

#25 – THE CHRISTMAS GIFT BY GEORGETTE HEYER

Friday, December 18, 2020

In a 1971 letter to her long-time agent, Joyce Weiner, Georgette Heyer recounted a short but delightful tale of her step-grandson's surprisingly nimble present... We share it here with you now, with thanks to Jennifer Kloester and her most extraordinary archive of extant Heyer documents:

2 January 1971

Dear Joyce,

[…]

Christmas was enlivened by the introduction into the household of Richard's [Georgette's son, Richard Rougier] present to his younger stepson, Noel, which was a baby chinchilla! A most entrancing little creature, which cast Noel into speechless ecstasies. It also provided Richard, Dominic [Richard's elder stepson], and me with a very nerve-racking hour, trying to catch it, and to put it into its hutch, what time Susie and her mother kept Noel occupied at the other end of the house! Richard and Dommy drove into Ledbury on Christmas Eve to collect it, and its hutch was placed, temporarily, in Richard's study.

Unfortunately, none of us three had realized the extraordinary agility of chinchillas!

Richard cautiously opened its travelling-box, expecting it to go straight into the hutch, but instead of doing this it leapt over Richard's hands, and defied capture for over an hour! My job was to guard the door against intruders, so that no one coming in should allow Sidney, the cat, to come in too! The poor little thing was quite unnerved by the unprecedented events of the day, of course. Its final refuge was behind the curtains which hang in front of Richard's very heavy desk, whence it made Distressful Noises, what time Richard and Dominic lay on their tummies, trying to cajole it into emerging!

It was Susie [Richard's first wife] who finally caught it, and put it into its hutch, where it very soon settled down, and, with perfect sangfroid, took a raisin out of Richard's fingers! When I left, it was rapidly developing into an enchanting pet, and Dominic, who is a good carpenter, was making two more hutches for it – one for travel, and the other for its London residence!

I hope 1971 will be a better year for you, and will end with my best wishes – in which Ronald [Georgette's husband] joins me.

Yours ever,

Georgette

———

Fifty years later, we most sincerely hope that 2021 is a better year for everyone!

Yours ever,

The Patronesses

~ | ~

AFTER GEORGETTE

Recommended Reading for the Heyer Fan

As an author of historical romance, Georgette Heyer is unmatched. But if you love Heyer, and have made your way through all of her works, what can you read next that might begin to compare? Here, the Patronesses make bold with some suggestions...

THE BLUE CASTLE BY L. M. MONTGOMERY (1926)

I adore her Anne books but my favourite L. M. Montgomery novel is *The Blue Castle*. Valancy's story never fails to move me; I love the humour and the romance in this surprising story. It's got a great twist and Barney Snaith is one of my all-time favourite heroes. If you haven't read it you have a treat in store. A delightful book. – *Jennifer Kloester*

CAKES AND ALE BY W. SOMERSET MAUGHAM (1930)

I love this book not only for its story and its many memorable characters, but also for its picture of English life between the Wars. It's a window into Georgette Heyer's world and the narrator's attitude to class is so much of its time and so very revealing! A marvellous satire about authors and the literary life. Delicious. – *Jennifer Kloester*

CATHERINE, CALLED BIRDY BY KAREN CUSHMAN (1995)

Set in late-13th century England, this journals the trials and tribulations (and occasional joys) of Birdy, the teen daughter of an uncouth minor noble of the time. Whether discussing the parasites that plague her, the maidenly occupations parasites that annoy her, or the forthcoming marriage that disgusts her, she is a feisty, hopeful yet strangely pragmatic soul. The book does not shy away from some of the less pleasant aspects of Medieval life, nor does it romanticize the period. Funny, immersive, upsetting and thought-provoking, it is YA, but so much more. – *Rachel Hyland*

CECILY BY CLARE DARCY (1972)

In the 1970s, American novelist Mary Deasy turned her hand to the Regency, with varying degrees of success. Her greatest accomplishment in the field (of her twelve attempts) is without a doubt Cecily, or A Young Lady of Fashion, the story of an impecunious young lady's attempts at gainful employment, and her self-appointed guardian's growing displeasure at her wilfulness. A fun romp. – *Rachel Hyland*

CRANFORD BY ELIZABETH GASKELL (1853)

Set in the titular small village in Victorian England, this book simmers with wit, satire and clever, incredibly amusing, dialogue. It is the 1850s and times are changing, but the residents of Cranford resist all thoughts of forsaking their prized genteel respectability. A new family in town brings new ideas, however, and soon the entrenched pillars of the community find themselves daring to think differently, and to seek their own happiness. A series of vignettes rather than a plot-driven novel, the whole nevertheless hangs together perfectly. Just delightful! – *Rachel Hyland*

THE CROSSING PLACES BY ELLY GRIFFITHS (2009)

Crime writer Elly Griffiths is clearly a big Heyer fan, for her fabulous series featuring forensic archaeologist Dr Ruth Galloway and police officer Harry Nelson is dotted with references to Heyer. Start with *The Crossing Places* and you will be transported to the Norfolk Coast, enjoy great dialogue, intriguing crimes, and fabulous romantic tension. Twelve books to give you satisfaction and reading pleasure for some time to come. I adore this series! – *Susannah Fullerton*

DADDY-LONG-LEGS BY JEAN WEBSTER (1912)

Spirited and intelligent orphan Judy wins the heart of a kindly elder gentleman she has never seen and sends him letters to update him on her progress at the exclusive women's college he is paying for. There, she meets, and is puzzled by, her close friend's handsome uncle. Written epistolary style with verve, humour and cleverness, it is easy to see why "Daddy-Long-Legs" fell for Judy; you will, too! – *Rachel Hyland*

THE ENDLESS STEPPE BY ESTHER HAUTZIG (1968)
A memoir describing a 10-year-old girl's exile from her home in Poland to Siberia, during WWII. At first Esther detests the place and endures poverty and loss. But when the time finally comes for them to go home, she discovers that she has become Siberian. A moving and powerful story. – *Susannah Fullerton*

A GIRL OF THE LIMBERLOST BY GENE STRATTON-PORTER (1909)
The enchanting story of Elnora Comstock, a marvellous and unique heroine. Her refuge is the Limberlost, an ancient swamp that once covered 13,000 acres of eastern Indiana. It is there that Elnora hope finds hope and love and a way to achieve her dreams. – *Jennifer Kloester*

LADY BETTY ACROSS THE WATER BY A.M. & C.N. WILLIAMSON (1906)
This engaging tale of a beautiful aristocrat introduced to wealthy 1900s New York society is simply delightful. Reading the naive yet insightful Lady Betty's journal, we see her become much feted in the very title-conscious confines of the nouveau riche elite. Betty's wonderment is very entertaining, as is the love story that unfolds quite unexpectedly. A forgotten gem. – *Rachel Hyland*

MISS BUNCLE'S BOOK BY D. E. STEVENSON (1934)
Every so often you come across a book that becomes an instant favourite; for me, such was this very funny novel. Miss Buncle is a maiden lady living in a small English village who, when money is tight, naively writes a novel about the only people and place she knows: her village, friends and neighbours. Though her motives are innocent, the consequences are beyond anything she could ever have imagined! This is one of my comfort reads; just the thing for a few hours' escape. – *Jennifer Kloester*

PERSUASION BY JANE AUSTEN (1817)
Many Heyer readers will know and love Jane Austen's novels and Persuasion is a favourite reread. Anne Elliot reminds me of several Heyeroines and there are elements of Austen's novel in several Heyer stories. Anne's journey to love and freedom from her awful family is compelling and the romance is perfection. – *Jennifer Kloester*

SECRET LIVES BY E. F. BENSON (1932)
This fabulous comedy of manners is about the residents of Durham Square, which is a respectable if not totally fashionable London address. We see their snobberies, their quarrels and reconciliations, and we discover that one of the residents of the square has been writing hugely popular romantic trash under the name of Rudolph da Vinci. There's a memorable cast of strong-willed women, an eccentric Vicar, an admirable butler, and some Pekinese dogs. This novel is laugh-out-loud funny! – *Susannah Fullerton*

THE WINTHROP WOMAN BY ANYA SETON (1958)
If you love the novels of Georgette Heyer, I can recommend The Winthrop Woman by Anya Seton. Published in 1958, it tells the story of Elizabeth Winthrop, niece of John Winthrop, one of the founders of Massachusetts. Bess is a fabulous heroine – warm, loving, feisty and independent. You learn lots of history as you read, and it's a memorable and enchanting novel. – *Susannah Fullerton*

THE YOUNG VISITERS BY DAISY ASHFORD (1919)
The tale of 17-year-old Ethel Monticue, invited to stay by "an elderly man of 42" who is "parshial to ladies", this novel's author was all of nine years old when she wrote it (hence the mistake spelling mistake in the title). The charm of this story comes from its eccentric grammar, its hilarious spelling and the naivety of its author. The narrative voice is distinctive, the story a wonderful commentary on Victorian High Society, and it is truly original. – *Susannah Fullerton*

~ | ~

THE READING ROOM

Books about Georgette Heyer, and her work

ACTING ON IMPULSE - CONTEMPORARY SHORT STORIES BY GEORGETTE HEYER
Eight contemporary shorts, and one historical tragedy, with commentary from experts collected for the first time.

COMPLETE TO A SHADE - A CELEBRATION OF GEORGETTE HEYER
Discover the enormous pleasure of Georgette Heyer in this collection of reminiscences from some of her most ardent admirers.

GEORGETTE HEYER: A CRITICAL RETROSPECTIVE
Fully indexed collection of articles on the popular author's works, addressing such subjects as "Georgette Heyer and the Uses of Regency" and the like.

GEORGETTE HEYER: BIOGRAPHY OF A BEST-SELLER BY JENNIFER KLOESTER
The ground-breaking biography of one of the world's best-loved and bestselling authors. Who was the real Georgette Heyer?

GEORGETTE HEYER'S REGENCY ENGLAND BY TERESA CHRIS
Join Judith Taverner, Annis Wychwood, the Prince Regent and more on a nostalgic, visual tour of Georgette Heyer's Regency England.

GEORGETTE HEYER'S REGENCY WORLD BY JENNIFER KLOESTER
The definitive guide for all fans of Georgette Heyer, Jane Austen, and the glittering Regency period.

THE GRAND TOUR - A TRAVEL GUIDE TO GEORGETTE HEYER'S LONDON
Visit important London landmarks, then and now, from hotels to gardens to the shops, homes and famous thoroughfares that were the playgrounds of the ton.

HEYER FOR BEGINNERS BY MAURA TAN
Contemporary fiction scholar and historical fiction naysayer Maura Tan takes a journey through Georgette Heyer, soon becoming a convert...

HEYER SOCIETY - ESSAYS ON THE LITERARY GENIUS OF GEORGETTE HEYER
Scholars, authors, bloggers and fans come together in a celebration of the works and worlds of Georgette Heyer.

THE PRIVATE WORLD OF GEORGETTE HEYER BY JOAN AIKEN HODGE
Lavishly illustrated, with extracts from her correspondence and references to her work, The Private World reveals a formidable and energetic woman.

READING HEYER: THE BLACK MOTH BY RACHEL HYLAND
An exploration of the great Georgette Heyer's seminal masterwork *The Black Moth*, taking a chapter-by-chapter look at the book's genius...

READING HEYER: POWDER AND PATCH BY RACHEL HYLAND
Bright, lively and incredibly detailed, this analysis exults in the novel's wit and historical nuance while also deploring the novel's heroine...

GEORGETTE HEYER'S BIBLIOGRAPHY

GEORGIAN NOVELS
The Black Moth (Constable, 1921)
The Transformation of Philip Jettan, aka *Powder and Patch* (Mills & Boon, 1923)
These Old Shades (William Heinemann, 1926)
The Masqueraders (William Heinemann, 1928)
Devil's Cub (William Heinemann, 1932)
The Convenient Marriage (William Heinemann, 1934)
The Talisman Ring (William Heinemann, 1936)
Faro's Daughter (William Heinemann, 1941)

REGENCY NOVELS
Regency Buck (William Heinemann, 1935)
An Infamous Army (William Heinemann, 1937)
The Spanish Bride (William Heinemann, 1940)
The Corinthian (William Heinemann, 1940)
Friday's Child (William Heinemann, 1944)
The Reluctant Widow (William Heinemann, 1946)
The Foundling (William Heinemann, 1948)
Arabella (William Heinemann, 1949)
The Grand Sophy (William Heinemann, 1950)
The Quiet Gentleman (William Heinemann, 1951)
Cotillion (William Heinemann, 1953)
The Toll-Gate (William Heinemann, 1954)
Bath Tangle (William Heinemann, 1955)
Sprig Muslin (William Heinemann, 1956)
April Lady (William Heinemann, 1957)
Sylvester, or the Wicked Uncle (William Heinemann, 1957)
Venetia (William Heinemann, 1958)
The Unknown Ajax (William Heinemann, 1959)
A Civil Contract (William Heinemann, 1961)
The Nonesuch (William Heinemann, 1962)
False Colours (The Bodley Head, 1963)
Frederica (The Bodley Head, 1965)
Black Sheep (The Bodley Head, 1966)
Cousin Kate (The Bodley Head, 1968)
Charity Girl (The Bodley Head, 1970)
Lady of Quality (The Bodley Head, 1972)

HISTORICAL NOVELS
The Great Roxhythe (Hutchinson, 1922)
Simon the Coldheart (William Heinemann, 1925)
Beauvallet (William Heinemann, 1929)
The Conqueror (William Heinemann, 1931)
Royal Escape (William Heinemann, 1938)
My Lord John (The Bodley Head, 1975)

CONTEMPORARY NOVELS
Instead of the Thorn (Hutchinson, 1923)
Helen (Longmans and Co., 1928)
Pastel (Longmans and Co., 1929)
Barren Corn (Longmans and Co., 1930)

DETECTIVE NOVELS
Footsteps in the Dark (Longmans and Co., 1932)
Why Shoot a Butler? (Longmans and Co., 1933)
The Unfinished Clue (Longmans and Co., 1934)
Death in the Stocks (Longmans and Co., 1935)
Behold, Here's Poison (Hodder & Stoughton, 1936)
They Found Him Dead (Hodder & Stoughton, 1937)
A Blunt Instrument (Hodder & Stoughton, 1938)
No Wind of Blame (Hodder & Stoughton, 1939)
Envious Casca (Hodder & Stoughton, 1941)
Penhallow (William Heinemann, 1942)
Duplicate Death (William Heinemann, 1951)
Detection Unlimited (William Heinemann, 1953)

SHORT STORY COLLECTIONS
Pistols for Two (William Heinemann, 1960)
Snowdrift and Other Stories (William Heinemann, 2016)
Acting on Impulse – Contemporary Short Stories by Georgette Heyer (Overlord, 2019)

JOIN THE INTERNATIONAL HEYER SOCIETY AT HEYERSOCIETY.COM

www.ingramcontent.com/pod-product-compliance
Lightning Source LLC
Chambersburg PA
CBHW081338080526
4458CB000178/2666